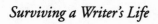

Surviving a Writer's Life

SUZANNE LIPSETT

Surviving a Writer's Life

HarperSanFrancisco
A Division of HarperCollins*Publishers*

Grateful acknowledgment is made to the following for permission to quote: Erica Jong for excerpts from her speech to The Authors Guild's California members, used by permission of the author; to the University of California Press for excerpts from Mary Barnard, *Sappho: A New Translation,* copyright © 1958 by the Regents of the University of California, © renewed 1984 by Mary Barnard. Reprinted with permission.

Illustrations by the author.

FIRST EDITION

Library of Congress Cataloging-in-Publication Data

Lipsett, Suzanne.
Surviving a writer's life / Suzanne Lipsett
lst ed.
p. cm.
ISBN 0–06–250657–9
ISBN 0–06–250658–7 (pbk)
1. Lipsett, Suzanne—Biography. 2. Novelists,
American—20th century—Biography.
3. Fiction—Authorship. I. Title.
PS3562.159Z469 1994   93–22857
813'.54—dc20   CIP

94 95 96 97 98 ❖ HAD 10 9 8 7 6 5 4 3 2 1

This edition is printed on acid-free paper that meets the American National Standards Institute Z39.48 Standard.

I wrote this book for my sons, Samuel Mitchell Rider and Evan Zachary Rider. But I dedicate it to my aunt, Victoria Lipsett, truth teller, and to all my dear book friends.

Thanks to Carolyn Heilbrun, whom I've never met but who taught me more about myself than I knew there was to learn. Both in title and content, this small book is a response to her exhilarating collection of essays, *Writing a Woman's Life.*

Also, thanks to Tom Grady and Caroline Pincus for the opportunity of a lifetime.

And a special note: This is not an autobiography. Nothing appears in it that is not tied directly to my life in books. Right from the start and with affection, I seek to reassure my second family that the life we shared together is not represented here.

Contents

Upon being asked, at the end of a long *Paris Review* interview, what writing had meant to him, Bernard Malamud responded,

"I'd be too moved to say."

When to Quit

I knew I was in trouble when I reflected on my reaction, which was spontaneous. Talk now, think later.

My dear friend had returned from a trip around the world. He had fabulous stories to tell—dramatic, exciting, exotic, some even hair-raising. He had eaten dog. He had helped to deliver a baby. He had unwittingly served as a courier in an international intrigue.

"My God, what fantastic material!" I shouted. "Material?" He was a contractor. "What do you mean, material?"

"I mean, what are you going to *do* with the trip? How are you going to use it?"

"*Do? Use?* You mean, write a 'What I Did on My Vacation' type thing? Hey, I've been finished with school for quite a few years now."

And I thought: "What a waste, what a tragedy. Those fantastic memories are locked inside this guy's head and he's just going to let them fade gradually away. Think of all that raw *art stuff* in there. Why did he even bother to go?"

The year-long trip, he told me, had cost him a cool $25,000. It took me several weeks to convince myself that by ignoring the opportunity to transform his experiences into art, this fellow hadn't flushed twenty-five grand down the toilet.

You mean life is more than material for books?

There's only one thing to do when you find yourself posing that question: stand up, walk away from your computer or your writing desk, and plunge your poor, steaming head into a bucket of ice water. Then lie down and let the sun dry you slowly while you think about nothing at all.

In editorial conferences, at writers' gatherings, at dinner parties over the years, I have met many people who would agree, with a laugh over coffee, that this is indeed the only response to the living-to-write syndrome. But I have either suspected or known for a fact that these very same people, after smiling and nodding amiably, have abruptly jumped up to return to a work-in-progress, perhaps even weaving the essence of our conversation into the manuscript. Year in, year out, these writers write with the hope, but never the reality, of readers. Routinely they suffer the kind of rejection that most people would do anything to avoid. They hear five, ten, fifteen different ways of saying that their work is bad, bad, bad; then they swallow it, absorb it, and keep on writing. And if you think it takes any less work to write a "bad" book than a "good" one, just try it sometime.

Often—dejected, defeated, and lonely as hell after days, weeks, months of clicking my words into a computer—I have wondered if I had fallen into this category of Writer Around the Bend. The speculative nature of the game makes it impossible to tell, and the mythology of publishing only fuels the addiction. William Kennedy–type stories, of writers laboring in obscurity until the eleventh hour; John Kennedy Toole–type stories, about suicides whose mothers obsess their offsprings' work into print; Barbara Pym–type stories, of writers on the down side of success suddenly snatched from oblivion by an astute and powerful critic; Amy Tan–type stories, of agents' discovery of literary jewels buried in tiny journals—all these are as coals to the eternal flame of the Writer Around the Bend.

J. D. Salinger's famous line, It's not over till the fat lady sings, never held any mystery for me. Writer to writer, Salinger was planting a seed of crazy belief at the turn of the sixties that has since spread into an impenetrable thicket of faith: as long as those little black marks are marching across white pages *somewhere*—in a drawer, in a trunk, in an attic—the possibility remains that they will ultimately find their audience. You can slip paper clips under the nails of the hundreds of thousands of aspiring writers, wannabe writers, grimly determined journeyman writers, and writers attempting to match or exceed an early success, and you'll never wipe out that faith. It's as tough, in the face of punishment, as religious fervor.

And the faithful form a virtual army of believers. You just cannot meet a person who has not entertained the fantasy of becoming a writer. You cannot find an institution of higher learning that is not running or developing a writer's conference. You cannot *miss* the writer's shelves in bookstores anymore—how to write believable characters, how to write snappy dialogue, how to construct a plot, how to write for television, how to write for the screen. . . . As publishers cut the length of their lists, so slush piles grow and grow.

We are swamping each other with stories. We are *drowning* each other with stories. We are telling each other the *same* stories over and over again—on the serious fiction shelves, in the literary journals, in the glossies, on the movie screen, on the daytime soaps. We are raising our unique voices and eliciting echoes from all around ourselves. And some of us—but we won't know who until you know when—are writing ourselves to death.

When does storytelling become not the noble effort to contribute to the world's culture and add to the body of evolving myth, but a desperate cry, a howl, to hear one's own voice above the din? When is it best simply to examine the impulse to speak up, to "transform," to "make use of" the "material" that is life for the possibility that it is a symptom rather than a calling? When might one suddenly shout "Enough!" to oneself, walk outside, and step fully into life? Is there, perhaps, a menopause of the mind, when the drive to create slowly loses power and one is finally enveloped by the simple luxury to *be*? In short, when is it time to quit?

Believe me, I ask these questions in earnest. Beneath them all lies one truly mysterious cluster of questions. They have risen up to haunt me intermittently for years, nearly always posed by a snide, somewhat impatient inner voice, a hip-cocking, eye-darting Miss Thing of the mind:

"Well, why *do* it then?" she demands. "I mean, why the burning passion to make up stories? Why drive yourself crazy? *Why write?*"

The short answer, and one that has usually worked to silence that ratty, upstart voice, is probably as accurate and definitive as all the reflections that make up this small book:

"Darling, it's all I can do."

The longer answer, like any regarding the reasons behind things human, involves a journey back in time. I always thought that if I could remember learning to read—that precise moment when marks of black ink on white paper suddenly jumped alive with meaning—I would understand a lot about myself and the storytelling impulse. And then one day, staring out my window and thinking about nothing at all, I nearly did.

Bookworms enter books and devour them, pages, paste, and bindings. They do not necessarily become smart in the process, but there is no doubt they are nourished by it. In the same way, I have been consuming books since the first one I read straight through, which was *Toby Tyler: Or Six Weeks in the Circus,* when I was five or six years old. I read it during a thunderous family meal at a relative's New York City apartment, and found to my intense relief when I finally looked up that I had missed dinner and my father was preparing to leave.

Since that day books have been food to me—sometimes, like baked potatoes, yielding little more than pure comfort, but often supplying the major nutrients in sustaining my inner life. In my next-to-darkest hours, books saved me. In my truly darkest hours, I could measure the seriousness: I no longer had the ability to take in a book. Like a tire spinning in a rut, my mind could only whir hopelessly over and over the words of a single sentence without getting snagged.

But I have never done my voracious reading to plan, and there are terrible holes in my literary knowledge that I dread will be accidentally revealed. Except for a mismanaged literature major in college during the clamorous sixties, when the outside world offered sufficient alternatives to reality, I have picked my own way through the complex world of books—often, especially in childhood, choosing those I read solely by their beckoning covers.

What this lifetime of reading, and reading fiction in particular, has yielded has been experience squared—vast reserves of memories, other people's memories, to consult for meaning in the face of life's myriad problems and puzzles. I have met many people who devour books and nourish their intuitive understanding this way, but I have never seen their pursuit of other people's worlds given fair due in print. I make this point as a disclaimer for readers who might have been drawn to a book on the writing life with expectations of authoritative, analytical literary commentary. Although much of my leisure and virtually all of my working life have been centered on books, I am not an intellectual and never have been: only, as both reader and writer, an intuitional, a responder from the deepest heart of the brain.

Books have nourished me literally as well as figuratively—I have made my living by editing other people's books since I graduated from college in 1965. And at a certain point, dismayingly late, I discovered that all along, by reading and editing constantly and by collaborating with life itself, I had become the thing that I had hardly dared wish I could be. I had become a writer myself. This book is a description and grateful celebration of that long, slow process of evolution.

In 1987 I had a frightening bout with breast cancer. In 1989 the disease recurred. It comes as news to most people—it was certainly news to me—that there is not only life after diagnosis of what medicine calls "terminal illnesses," but there is life after recurrence. And in a very real sense it is life laid bare—a virtual laboratory for a writer.

Although I consider it fair to warn readers who might be illness-phobic (and who isn't?) that disease and its impact arise as topics here, this is not a book about cancer. Like most people of forty-nine, I have been baptized many times by the cold waters of reality, and all those immersions have contributed directly to my gradual evolution into a writer. Still, being dangled over the abyss has caused my last hesitancies regarding my identity as an artist to melt away. Ironically cancer has made me, for better or worse, fully a writer, and has shown me something wonderful: that my life has a shape. In that shape is meaning, and meaning—as any dedicated bookworm knows—is the nutrient in books.

One more note: Seeing the many *I*'s and *me*'s and *my*'s scattered across these pages strikes terror in my fiction writer's heart. About every third day as I wrote these pieces, I considered the strategy of recasting the whole book into the third person so I could hide behind a barricade of *she*'s and *her*'s. But the subtext of this small book, and the soil in which it is rooted, is authenticity and the vitality and value it brings to the written word. So I've waited out the doubt that has risen up like hot flashes. Here is my answer to the asker within me who occasionally, and with such devastating directness, demands to know, for God's sake, why write? It is not meant to be an autobiography, but rather an account of how—and why—the first impulses toward self-expression can gain force to become a life's work. And yet there has been no way to the truth, *this* truth anyhow, except through the thicket of my own point of view. For better or worse, this is my honest story. No good—no way—to try to duck out of it now.

TILLING

ONE

The Elephant's Shadow

In 1968, in Kenya, I was charged by an elephant. I was on my first trip abroad, I was scared all the time, and my main job throughout the journey was to conceal from my traveling companions the stomach-shaking anxiety elicited in me by the beautiful, vast savannas of East Africa. On a dusty, hot—and lonely—red road through a national game reserve, our car, a tiny, tough Rover, disturbed a rogue elephant at his grazing. He wheeled at our approach, he waved his ears, he snuffled and snorted and rocked back and forth. His agitation was obvious and his physical size terrifying. The top of the car barely reached his chest. Had he taken a step or two in our direction, his shadow would have completely engulfed our little wheeled carapace. He threatened to do so and trumpeted. He surged forward, lifted his trunk in earnest, and trumpeted loudly again.

"He's bluffing," said my boyfriend. We sat side by side on the edge of the backseat—he in excitement, me in alarm. We had hitched this ride with an English couple from a town outside the reserve. The Boyfriend rolled down the window and the smell of the savanna whooshed into the car along with something richer, meatier: elephant.

"Quite an effective bluff," said our driver, a dentist, whose hands gripped the wheel. Distractedly he had slowed the car nearly to a halt at the sight of the raging bull. "I'm impressed."

Oh, shit, I was thinking. I might cry. In full terror of death by crushing, I still felt irritated at the need to conceal my girlish nerves from the young, handsome, fearless man beside me. As the dentist began to inch by the furious elephant as quietly as possible while rattling along in fourth gear—I could see he didn't dare to risk the noise of shifting to first—I let the full array of emotions pass through me: fright, respect, anger at the intrusion and threatening humiliation, fascination at the absolute maleness of the beast expressed to the fullest degree, attraction to the protective force it exuded and to an unmistakable impression of kindness, and a tiredness that signaled resignation to the clearly superior power.

The moment passed. One more trumpet, one more wave of the heavy, sail-shaped ears, and the fabulous, saggy old grayskin rocked away and resumed the languid rubbing of his tusks against a tree. The dentist floored it and he, his wife, and I began literally to scream with relieved laughter. The Boyfriend, who had traveled much in Africa and had seen it all when it came to animals, retained his dignity in silence.

The crazy ball of feelings that elephant brought up in me—fear and irritation mixed with respect and awe—was as familiar as the inside of my own skin. It had risen up all my life any time my father trumpeted his displeasure, which was often. Those moments occurred throughout our stormy life together as unpredictably as the appearance of an elephant suddenly stepping out of a dense grove of trees. My father's skin was saggy, his cheeks and body were soft, but he had a fierceness that vied with a nearly palpable desire simply to sit peacefully on and on in a chair without being disturbed. He threw temper tantrums at me all though my childhood and until the last year of his life, when I was forty. But beneath these great displays lay a protective love as unshakable as the bonds of animal instinct. He always saw in me the beginnings of an artist. With a loyalty that I still find amazing, he did everything he could to buffer me against the random blows of life until I could look below the surface of myself and see those beginnings too.

It took me more than three and a half decades to dig out of my father the details of my mother's death. By the time he was finally willing to allow the dreaded truth into his consciousness, he had forgotten nearly everything. It had happened, after all, thirty-six years before. It had risen up unexpectedly and severed past from future—one moment we were a family of three looking forward to a newborn who would complete the quartet, the next there was only my father and me; my mother and the promised baby were gone.

Upon the shock and awfulness of this unanticipated event my father had slammed the door with all the tremendous force of his personality, a rogue elephant force that, when applied to a door, would permanently wedge the thing shut. In most other ways, he gradually regained his vitality and vast appetite for life. But this death, these two deaths, became a terrible secret that we had somehow agreed—he silently but commandingly, me in some terror—to keep, even from each other. When I finally gained the courage, it took the most careful probing on my part, and the risk of hitting a nerve, to get even the little that was left in his memory out of him that last year. By then, although we were not to mention this either, he was close to death himself.

I remember him propped on the couch in a special way that the home-care nurse had devised, for disease had spread to his bones and the mere pressure of his body weight could exhaust him. I had to ask gently, and yet I had to ask. What had happened to my mother? Why had she died? What had happened? All I knew was that she had died in childbirth when I was four and half, and I had no memory of her whatsoever. About three years later, when I was seven, my father had remarried, a new family had been started, and I was always the odd one after that. I never fit, I was unpredictable, "artistic." I was different and my mother had died and I had no memory of her. Somehow that left me rudderless—what was I supposed to be? How was I supposed to start?

"It was a normal pregnancy," he said, staring at the blank television screen. He had always been such a big man that disease had left him, though thinner, looking fairly fit. There was still a hint of the robust man in the moony roundness of his face, and the dapper Thin Man mustache went further still in disguising the illness with a well-calibrated touch of class. "There was never a hint of anything wrong, Sugar. She, uh, Elynore . . . your mother—" waves of embarrassment assailed us both, and I had to struggle to keep my eyes steady. He looked away, eyes shifting sideways from the blank screen. Mentioning her, mentioning her name, mentioning her name in the same sentence with a reference to myself—these were thirty-six-year-old taboos.

"What happened? Exactly?"

"Shug, *Shug,* it was so *long* ago. It's close to forty years already. How can I remember every detail?"

"Not every," I told him. "Not every detail. Just one or two. Some. Just tell me what you can."

He sighed a long, shuddering sigh. "She died, that's all. One minute the door to her hospital room was open, the next, it was closed. That's all."

"That's all you can remember?"

"Shug, what are you doing to me? That's all there *was.*"

His eyes settled on the television and he pressed the remote control. The screen burst into life with a crack, and that was the end of that.

"*Dad!*" I begged.

"It was very sad," he told Ted Koppel. "It was terribly, terribly sad. . . . "

It was part of the family mythology that in the nights following my mother's death my father had to put an end to my padding into his bedroom and crawling into bed with him. He never spoke of my mother; nor did my Aunt Sylvia and my grandmother, her sister and mother, who lived in the flat downstairs. But he told me many times how I would creep into his room in the night. "Then came the longest night of my life," he would say, "when I had to let you cry it out. No more. You were a big girl, nearly five. So I made up my mind and I waited. And when you came in, in the night, I walked you back. And when you cried and came out, I walked you back. Then I sat in my chair, because I couldn't go to sleep, and you cried through the whole night, the *whole* night. But I knew if you cried through the whole of one night, you would never cry again. And you would never come in asking to sleep in my bed again. And I was right."

For many years, when I hoped to excavate from my memory a scrap of information, a detail, or a feeling related to my mother, instead would rise a picture of that house on Granger Place in Buffalo, New York. In the upstairs flat would be my father in his robe, sitting in his nubby, over-stuffed green chair, his feet in leather slippers out in front of him on the ottoman that had claws.

In the downstairs flat would be Aunt Sylvia, tall and buck-toothed, kind, brutally shy, and my grandma, a silent rock of grief, lying in their beds, listening. My father had barred all tears of grief in my presence; this fact too entered the small body of myth passed down to me. Surely they never spoke to me of that night, and as far as I know my aunt and grandmother never spoke of my mother's life, perhaps not even to each other. And my father was right. After that night I myself very nearly never cried again.

That's the way you render a whole life a secret, rewrite reality, and ensure the collusion of others: with the silence of the elephant and the sheer force of his will. With never a reference made to my mother for thirty-six years, with all the photographs snatched up and hidden, with all the accoutrements of her life—her clothes, her books, her *things,* whatever they might have been—spirited away forever, any memories these scraps and bits might have triggered in me sank away.

Down below the surface these shadowy protomemories mingled with the earliest stirrings of imagination and the first impulses to create. There, as early as that, they slowly became the stories I would have the courage to tell only decades later. They grew silently in the close, hot closet of my deepest mind, like mushrooms in the dark.

I was in the tub, being given a bath. My father, ever struggling with his somewhat puritanical dignity to be both mother and father, stood half-turned away from me, towering over the tub. My head was a froth of lather; in the clumsy way of children, I'd been scrubbing it myself. "Here," said my father, handing over the bar of soap. "Here, Sugar. Wash between your legs."

I was five. I had, perhaps, just had soap in my eyes, though he had carefully scraped my forehead clean of suds. I took the soap but objected, "No, it hurts," thinking how soap had gone up inside before and burned like it burned the eyes.

"Wash," he intoned—the elephant rumbled.

"Daddy, it hurts."

"It doesn't. It won't hurt. You need to be clean there."

"Daddy, it's going to hurt." Tears threatened.

"Wash." He took the soap and rubbed it on the washcloth. Turning his back on me, he held the cloth out behind him over the tub. "Up there. Inside."

I did, and for a minute I thought it was going to be all right. After all, he *said* it was going to be all right. But then the burn began to build like a siren approaching from far away. The betrayal brought *outrage*—and then a nearly indelible impulse to protect him from the fact that he was wrong. I squelched hurt, angry words in my throat. So I was constricted at both places, top and bottom, and in between was the knowledge, rapidly growing like a plant captured by a time-lapse camera, that his reality was as real as mine but *different.*

"That wasn't so bad, was it?" he asked me, holding out his hand for the washcloth. With the words a lump in my throat, I shook my head. He had me stand up and he rinsed me all over with a cup and then lifted me out onto the bath mat and wrapped me in a white towel.

So, very young, I had a second secret, my first apart from him, hidden inside my body between two tightly squeezed openings. The secret was a knowledge that about myself and my body and the inner recesses of my mind I could be right and my father wrong. Woven through it were threads of emotion that were utterly mine. And though

I clung to my father like a barnacle to a piling, for many years I kept this special knowledge, this privacy, tightly closed away, down in the mulch with my other secrets.

Driving near our house in Buffalo, we came to an intersection. I know it was in a wealthy part of town: the houses were large and set back from the street. Little statues of black coach boys in livery, with rings for carriage reins, stood along the curbs. I can call them up now from memory and shake my head at the ludicrous affectations of the rich, but at the time I thought they were dolls put out on the curb for children's pleasure. It must have been fall or spring, for I was wearing a coat, but the trees I could see around us were leafed out, forming a canopy above the street.

What had I said to bring on the reaction from my father that would inscribe itself like the word of God upon the tablets of my memory? He twisted his body away from the steering wheel and leaned over me with his face close to mine—his doughy, soft, mushy face with the carefully trimmed mustache and the heavily lashed deep blue eyes.

"There is one thing I hate," he said, in a voice full of warning, "and that is a liar."

Though I no longer remember my terrible infraction, I can still recall the feel of my eyes opening wider and my face growing heavy with fear. He could *hate* me, I thought— if I lied again, even by accident, he could *hate* me. Before the car drove on past the stop sign, I vowed solemnly always to tell the truth.

So at my father's knee, or at least sitting docilely beside him, I learned at age five that parts of life can sink away out of sight and even out of memory if no one sets them in words, witnessing their existence. I learned too that I had a truth that was mine alone, separated by the walls of my mind from the quick intelligence of my father. And I learned, in a single indelible moment that left me quaking and promising, that despite the secret dwelling below all language, where my mother's life and death lay pressed down in the dark, to remain worthy of love I would have to tell the truth. Before I was six, I had all the pieces but one of a storyteller's inexplicable mind.

The missing piece came to me when I was sixteen, with all the high drama of adolescence. We had moved from the East Coast out to California. A new picture-perfect family had been forming—all shiny and bright, playing board games after dinner—right under my outsider's nose. For years not a word, not a syllable, had been spoken, not even a half-breathed mistake had been made to break the taboo against mentioning the other lives my father and I had shared—first with my mother and then alone together. And yet I thought about them every day, wishing to the point of pain that I could dredge up a single memory of the woman who might have hinted at the woman I was going to be. And daily I fended off blasts of panic at the thought that a person, *any* person, could disappear so completely.

That year, my junior year in high school, I took a creative writing class, in which the best writers—three very different boys—were all named Mike. The first, our star, wrote stories sharp as blades that slid right into your brain. The particulars are gone now, but I do remember sitting in a schoolroom in the suburban San Fernando Valley, nearly unconscious with the weight of the smoggy heat on a blistering afternoon, listening to this boy, Mike, read a story he'd knocked off the night before. I remember alertness and respect dawning together—the story woke me up and I felt its power. I'm honestly surprised I never heard of him again. And what I wouldn't give to sit in now on some of those intense, often hilarious fifty-minute discussions, punctuated by sharp laughter, on what exactly fiction was and what we were doing when we read and wrote it.

Another Mike—a man-sized boy who was going to be a priest—wrote fabulous stories of a different sort: minute investigations of Catholic family life that seemed as exotic and obscure to me, a Jewish girl in culture and upbringing if not in practice, as an aborigine tribe depicted in the *National Geographic*. It was from him that many of the laugh blasts emanated, for his commitment to join the priesthood was coupled with a wickedly quick and dirty wit, and he howled and turned red in the face at his own jokes. He was a huge boy, even in the eleventh grade probably close to two hundred and twenty pounds and pear-shaped, and by all laws of stereotypes he should have been the target of merciless teasing. He may well have been, in fact, but he was so quick and deadly with his retorts, and they always had such a hilarious spin, that at least in this class he was considered a major talent.

The third Mike was a sexually compelling boy. Though I was immune to his appeal at the time, I did sense, in the slow eyes and drawling voice, his lazy eroticism and his comfortable familiarity with it. It was 1960, and his group was known in the school for being something like beatniks. They listened to *Word Jazz* and read *Howl* and never attended a "function." Long after graduation, I realized it was marijuana that had set his group apart, and that had probably invested his stories with the soft, smoky quality that made them fade from my memory. Marijuana in high school in 1960—easy enough to recognize the signs now, looking back, but then all my rebellion was tied up in smoking cigarettes. Marijuana never crossed my mind.

I was fourth in the class, I think, behind the Mikes. One day I wrote my first "after" story—now I can see that I have been writing about aftermaths of trauma ever since. This was a lugubrious little affair called "After the Funeral." It was told from the viewpoint of a four-year-old girl moving in and among a party of adults who stood and talked low and even cried above her head. She was scared and agitated at the sight and sound of so much free-flowing emotion, so she finally took it upon herself to leave—no one was paying her much attention—and put herself to bed. There she lay awaiting her mama, whom she hadn't seen in a while.

It was an oppressive story, I admit, but the teacher liked it. Now, for years I've remembered the event this way: She liked it so much she decided to have it published in the school paper as a surprise, and she had advance copies mailed to my family so they could celebrate the honor. But as I write this, it seems more likely that indeed I knew it would be in the paper, and perhaps I even brought the advance copies home. For the truth of truths—crazy as it seems—is that I considered this story a work of pure imagination with no connection to myself or my own biography. It was a made-up girl at a made-up wake, an exercise in point of view, a fiction.

The scene that story triggered is a virtual blur of high feeling, shouted explanations, agitated arguing and explaining and misunderstanding and apologizing in first one room, then another, of our long, skinny, ranch-style house. "I want you to know I *never,* I absolutely *never* permitted a tear to be shed in your presence," my father told me. "If I saw someone in our flat threatening to cry, that was *that,* they were downstairs, *out.*" He trumpeted with alarm at the realization that I had misremembered.

"But it's just a story. It wasn't supposed to be *us,*" I stammered, horrified that I had triggered this vast outpouring.

But my father was unstoppable, and from this steadfast rock whose utter control I depended upon poured a geyser of grief and uncertainty. "Perhaps I did wrong," he told me, "because you've become so strange and disrespectful. But I wouldn't let them near you if they talked about your mother, and I wouldn't let them near you if they cried."

"Who? Who?"

"Anybody, nobody. Perhaps I did the wrong thing with you," he said to me, his eyes terribly troubled. "But, you know, Shug, I did what I thought I had to do. I did the best I could."

I flew to my room, where echoes of that old, suppressed life came to me in the chenille of the spreads on the twin beds. On my side, my cheek pressed hard against the little cotton knobs, I took down a book and dove in headfirst, pulling the story up over me. I was scalded by the dose of raw feeling my little fiction—"only a story"—had let loose in the house.

So it was that I learned how, in both writer and reader, fiction writing unleashes the truth in all its formidable power. This tool was so potent that phantoms composed only of words, mere marks on a page, could shatter the orderly calm of suburban family life. Without knowing of my own decision, I laid the tool aside; I didn't even try to write fiction again for many years. Perhaps I feared the thing going off in my face. At any rate, I had no desire to bring the old elephant down.

PLANTING

TWO

Raw Material

Doors slamming on doors.

You know how in hotel suites sometimes you open a door to the adjoining room only to find another door shut tight? After the debacle of the short story, my father slammed the door on our former life once more, and I slammed the door on that blessed world where the three Mikes and I had been looking for ways to dazzle each other with words. I slammed, wheeled, and dove into life on my own, off to college in Berkeley. Sounds brisk and well-scrubbed—"off to college." But it was the beginning of the sixties and, to complete the diving metaphor, I was lucky as I plunged in headfirst that there was water in the pool—not much, but some, and draining fast.

I learned to write academic English in the daytime. At night I went dancing in a place called the Steppenwolf—a name appropriate to the tenor of the times, considering Hermann Hesse's grip on students who were on their way to full-blown psychedelia. Each week by Thursday this narrow, stifling bar in the Berkeley flatlands was jammed tight with people fiercely seeking a good time or something like it: oblivion with a twist.

The twist was racial tension, turned up a few notches at night and fueled by alcohol and music.

There is no way that place could have had a license for dancing. In the wasteland of San Pablo Avenue, stuck in among credit furniture warehouses, thrift shops, and a weird, cavernous market that sold dented canned goods, the Steppenwolf was a tinderbox waiting for a spark. But it was a tinderbox that a big, invisible hand could have been shaking from the outside, because everybody in it, cheek to jowl, butt to belly, thigh to thigh, hand to crotch, and front to backside, was jumping and dancing to the thundering music. An alien might have wondered what terrible affliction had trapped us all in that box, or perhaps would have recorded it as a religious rite because it looked—and felt— like an ecstatic frenzy, and it was.

I went there with friends, but you couldn't drink or talk together, you could only dance. Even if you didn't dance you danced—the place took you with it. I had never been much of a dancer before and haven't been one since, but I danced at the Steppenwolf, danced with strangers and danced alone and danced occasionally with the people I knew, sometimes kissing at the height of a record ones I would have been too shy to speak to in daylight. The place was usually so packed by midnight that people started dancing on tables, and even that higher level was so crowded it might have satisfied the hopes of any bar owner on its own.

I danced on tables too. I didn't know what I was doing or how to act—nobody knew how to act in those days, or what we were playing with. Perhaps if the place had been less crowded we all would have seen that the young black men and women from the Oakland neighborhoods and the white university students freshly released from the suburbs of America, their newly evolving identities as fragile and changeable as their clothes, were circling and staring at each other with distrust and curiosity, with ignorance and a thirst for experience, and with emotions boiling down under that haven't any names. Some of the feelings were idle, some mysterious and deeper than the deepest spoken thought. One night I came home from oblivion with a series of clean, nearly bloodless razor cuts laddering up my thigh.

My daylight hours could not have been more different. At the university I was wandering in a desert that just skirted an oasis, and the oasis was the few classes offered in writing. Here and there, without my control, the drumming passion of those nighttime forays merged with my studies, and an analytic paper became an all-night orgy of casting hot thoughts into words. Invariably, though, I'd be stung in those epiphanies by the arch marginal notes of a seedy teaching assistant—"Oh, *really*? Do we *care*?" Or the death sentence: "Subjective!" accompanied by an angry slash. Gradually I learned how to read so that books entered my head and stayed there, never sinking down to the place where I could savor their meaning. If books had been rooms for me before, now they were large, echoing public buildings, cold, hard-surfaced monuments full of strangers. The echoes of voices made such a racket that an authentic emotional response to the art housed there was impossible.

At work, on the Cal Berkeley campus, I wrote lazy professors' books for a clerk-typist's pay. I still can't look at a textbook without wondering what poor student, on subsistence pay, really wrote it. But I had a small office to myself, and the company was good. There was certainly more happening there than in my lonely little studio apartment, where the guy across the street and I often stared into each other's windows: we were both big readers and both read in bed, though we never spoke on the street. That guy, my books, and a wrong number who became a frequent caller made up a good percentage of my social life. The rest entailed a group house mired in marijuana and music: we had barbecues and then sank to the floor under the weight of our heads, floating as if at the bottom of the sea through the music of Bob Dylan, Jimi Hendrix, the Band, and the Rolling Stones.

One day, blasting suddenly out of a tunnel I had barely known there, life came barreling at me like a freight train. The irony is, as I ponder it now, that train was to scoop me up and carry me even farther off my course than I had fallen on my own. The track eventually looped out of the country and completely around the world, but—so odd, so strangely lucky in a horrible way—eventually and perhaps inevitably that runaway train carried me home to myself, to my real life's work, to those doors upon doors in my mind.

The day was a Thursday, July 3. It was deathly hot. I was wearing a short dress of a synthetic silky fabric, flower-printed, and my thighs stuck to my chair. I wore patent leather shoes with no hose—too hot. This was nearly thirty years ago, and I can still remember how the four buttons at the top of the dress in back fitted through loops of fabric and left little gaps. At two or so in the sultry afternoon heat, I gave up on the article I was trying to create from my boss's single page of notes and left to go to the bathroom, outside the department lobby and down the hall.

When I emerged from the stall and stepped to the sink to wash my hands, I looked up to see a man—in his late twenties, early thirties, wearing black and standing straight up against the tile wall, staring at me in the mirror. Was he a workman, a plumber? Had he forgotten to put the yellow "closed" sign on the door and had I surprised him at his work? Embarrassed, I laughed—honestly, I can still hear my laughter ringing against the tiles.

Two strides and he stood behind me, breathing hotly on my neck. "Shut up," he said, and in the mirror I saw the muzzle of a gray-blue gun pushed into my hair just above my ear, saw it in the mirror and felt it, but—this was the beginning of the bizarre perceptual disjointedness that characterized the whole experience—as two separate events, remembered separately.

It had to be a toy, I thought. I don't believe I had ever seen a real gun before, except snapped into a policeman's holster. My mind told me, based on past experience, it *had* to be a toy.

"Shut up," he said again, though I couldn't have made a sound.

Behind us was a door. He pushed the gun harder into my head, not so it hurt, but so it nudged me in the direction of the door. He flung it open, and there was the cell we would occupy together for long, tangled hours—a tiny room with a bed: a state law required such amenities in all workplace women's rooms. It contained a cot for women with cramps and a cruel gray blanket.

The man put me in there at the end of his gun and closed the door behind him. "Down, down," he said, but then changed his mind and, signaling with his gun, had me take off my clothes. In a moment of pure comedy, if comedy is a burst of the unexpected that doesn't kill anybody, he had to help me take the dress off over my head and lay it down at the end of the bed. As if somebody had just shoved a baby into his arms and run away, the incongruity of my silky, flowery summer dress in his hands rendered him momentarily ridiculous—not that I was laughing now. I lay back down on the scratchy blanket, my legs straight out in front of me, and then flew up to the right-hand corner of the tiny little room to watch.

It was then that the man began to talk.

Thirty years, and I can remember how the buttons fastened on my dress, and I can remember that the man talked nonstop for as long as it took—which was long, which was long—I can remember that what he said made me know he was completely and permanently crazy, swinging in arcs from fantasy to reality and back again into some fully peopled scenario in his mind. I can remember the sound of his voice as he spoke, and how it worked its way into anger and then back to a kind of purring thoughtfulness, and I can remember how we both appeared from my odd vantage point on the ceiling as he poked me here and there and everywhere with his gun and told me what to do next. And I can even remember how I thought that the worst thing of all was that I still had on my patent leather shoes and how they seemed so sad. I can remember the up and down of his voice, its arcs, but I can't remember a thing that crazy man said.

It did take forever, so long in fact, requiring so many changing strategies and separate operations, that I had to assume that at the moment of climax he would shoot me. He said he would shoot me, he promised to shoot me, and the calm thing up in the corner of the room received the news with neutrality and patience.

But all of a sudden he was up and on his feet and full of warning: he warned me not to move for twenty minutes or or or or—and then he was gone. The thing in the corner watched the thing on the bed comply—second followed second followed second until both things at once realized that he was gone, fled, probably out of the building and on the street by now, and the thing at the ceiling reentered the body and I was whole again.

The return was accomplished just as I was pondering how I might sense, without benefit of a watch, that the twenty minutes had passed. With my world rent, how was I to know whether twenty seconds, twenty minutes, twenty hours, or years, or eons had passed? I saw that it was impossible, and that it had been just a ruse anyway—he had conditioned me with that gun to obey, but the gun was gone now and I got up.

Back in my department, I found my friend Gina, the receptionist.

"Where *have* you been?" she drawled, high-pitched. She was from Texas, and screamed sometimes.

"Call the police," I commanded.

"What, what?"

"Call the police," I told her, and she did.

So that Thursday, before work, I had had no warning as I was slipping on my dress and my patent leather shoes that before the workday ended I was to have every imaginable form of sexual intercourse with one stranger, be grilled with the greatest rigor by another, be skewered in the hospital by several more with sharp metal instruments and finally made to cry, if briefly, before being shown the door to wind up alone and changed forever on the street. It was the back door of Herrick Hospital, near the emergency entrance, and if I had been aware of my loneliness night after night in my room, I was still unprepared for loneliness as it is experienced in the daylight by one who has been taken past the reach of human kindness.

Because I was. I stood and watched people walk past me. I felt the heat of the July afternoon pounding me so that my hair hung damp and lank into my eyes. I felt a slick of lubricant on the inside of my thighs and a burning—like soap!—in my poor handled and rehandled crotch.

I was lonelier than I'd ever been as an out-of-whack student lacking a clear direction. But as I stood outside the back door of Herrick Hospital, released into the street after a silent pelvic exam, I felt the compulsion to write, long out of use, kick in like a high-power gear. It would be ten years before I could even *say* the word *rape,* and by that time I would have lived—luckily—through an eerie double replay of the whole incident, when two women-hating "magazine salesmen" pushed into my house. This time the punishment for being in the wrong place (home) at the wrong time (two o'clock in the afternoon) came with a beating that left much of my body and especially my face the royal purple and yellow of an overripe plum. It took many years after that to recover from the dismay and peculiar embarrassment at having had such a thing happen to me *twice.* But now I wonder how many who were young and free in those crazy, hell-bent years reached thirty without having physically experienced the perils of the times.

If ever a writer had her first book pounded into her, I was it. In a crazy way, I told myself, I had been given a privileged view of something close to the heart of darkness. If only I could climb outside it to that calm observing place where I had floated at the time. Not as therapy, mind you. Not to exorcize, but to *make use.* The urge—the unspeakably *urgent* urge—was to transform these raw experiences into something other, something *more,* something that might even, in a way as yet unimaginable to me, flash with a kind of beauty.

But I couldn't do it. I must have tried fifty or sixty times to transform those terrible encounters into something they weren't, every failing time managing no more than a superficial rendering of an event seen far-off, as if through a paper tube. I found new meaning in the tired metaphor of life as an onion: these overfull life experiences I was trying to release onto the page seemed made up of layer upon layer of nearly transparent tissue, tissue that cracked and tore at a too-heavy touch. Writing and rewriting, my frustration grew at being unable to slice straight through to the heart, and the meaning, of the matter.

What I didn't know then was that the very events were growing new skins as fast as I could peel the old ones away. As to the meaning of these random events, the hidden heart within them that I could liberate and use, there was none—only random hatred, dressed up in city clothes.

THREE

Gaining Distance

Empathy. 1: the imaginative projection of a
subjective state . . . into an object so that the object
appears to be infused with it . . . (without empathy
an artistic emotion is purely intellectual and
associative—W. H. Wright) 2: the capacity for
participating in or a vicarious experience of another's
feelings, volitions, or ideas (the goal of all reading is
empathy with the content and the spirit of the
material read—Stella Center).

Webster's Third New International Dictionary

Empathy is the writer's, and especially the fiction writer's, stock in trade. Without it we would have
nothing but journals and autobiographies, and thin ones at
that, in which to explore the emotional realities of others.
And those of us with the urge to write would remain
trapped in the anterooms between our own deepest truths
and the pulsing, deep-breathing, song-singing world.

Though at twenty-four and supremely untraveled I was not yet aware of it, traveling across national borders is a school for empathy. Now I see that somehow the accidents of my life matched the need I had, if I ever wished to become a writer, to break free of my own life and end what long afterwards I came to regard as the tyranny of autobiography.

At the time, however, in the now-distant sixties, I had no sense of embarking on the next phase of my literary education. In a single evening, surrounded by a hundred false starts crumpled into balls around my chair, I saw through to the hollow center of what I was trying to do—somehow to make a story out of an experience, rape, that I was only longing to forget. I gave up, packed up my simple life on Grove Street in Berkeley, and ran.

There *was* a life out there, a clamorous one. Not just I, but many (most?) students then—surely most students in Berkeley, California—were ricocheting from shard to shard of a culture fragmenting under the weight of racism and the Vietnam war. The boys I knew were targeted by the draft and—horrified, *outraged,* at the idea of taking up arms and blindly shooting—they had either burrowed more deeply into the liberal arts or, as I suddenly longed to do, taken off running. Briefly I considered the kind invitation of a concerned friend to join him in Toronto, where he was sitting out the war. He had heard of the nightmare assault I'd been through and offered just the kind of sympathy I was unable to receive. I chose instead to pick up the threads of a long, intermittent romance—replete with all the emotional encumbrances that ambiguous word connotes—that had been interrupted similarly by the threat of the draft. In the manner of many gentle suburban boys, the Boyfriend was performing alternative service via the Peace Corps in Somalia. Moving from the San Fernando Valley to Berkeley and straight into the sixties had been my first trip on my own. Fleeing Berkeley on an impulse to join my friend at the end of his tour in Mogadiscio, and seemingly traveling back in time to the fourteenth century, was my second.

I awoke at dawn on the flight across the breadth of Africa to see a dry ocean bed, an endless pan of parched and cracked desert, tinged rose by a small, mean-red sun. Here and there was a track or a path—perhaps a road— slicing through the crust and stretching to nowhere. There were no towns, no settlements, nothing for hours. The only motion was the gradual change in hue, from the pink tones to an angrier orange, picked up less from the sun than the land itself, with great swathes of yellows and grays pounded into paleness by the brutal rising sun.

The desert ended quite suddenly, with only a line of trees, then another strip of sand, then more trees, a moving white fringe, and the sea. The Indian Ocean was a vision of blue that eased the mind. The plane tilted on its wing and made a fluid downward arc, and there it was—a city on the coast composed of haphazard stacks of square white habitations and red roads. As we descended I saw the dhows— fishing boats that had remained unchanged in style for centuries—and little donkeys on the city's unpaved roads.

As soon as I felt the grip of my old beau's hand on the back of my neck, ostensibly steering me through the quonset hut that was Somalia's international airport, I knew that, physically close as we would be for the duration of the months-long trip we had planned along the hippie trail, I was alone in Mogadiscio. The heat burned through my sandals. The heat burned my hair. The heat seemed to envelop me and squeeze, causing sweat to run down my body continually, front and back. I hoisted my bags onto the borrowed, open jeep and tried to shake from my mind the image of the thousands and thousands of miles of empty desert I had crossed in the night. Why, this tiny collection of stuccoed boxes set close up to the sea was itself more alone than I ever thought a city could be. Ships came, but how often? The flight from Rome arrived once a day. I felt the emptiness of the space that stretched behind the jeep as we drove toward the sea and the town. No wonder that in the intervening years the country has all but turned to dust under the steady pressure of famine, drought, and civil war. With terrible irony, Somalia's remoteness to Americans has dissolved in the face of famine and relentless tribal hatred, and as I write this, media images of starving Somalis have become the ghosts that shoot through our attempts to believe that all, on earth, is well.

Our home was to be a small collection of rooms at the top of an ancient white building. Silently I followed my friend up a steep staircase on the structure's outside wall. Even the width and height of the stairs were calibrated to some exotic, historical standard, and I felt vertigo pulling from the ground as we ascended without benefit of a railing. Just as it began to get too high, the stairs twisted in through a dark opening in the wall, and the cool, delicious blackness brought me instantly to my senses.

The rooms were empty but for a bed and a couch, and outside the main room was a door to the roof. In air blown clean by the ocean breeze, I stood above the city and let my eyes travel from level to level—building blocks, none of matching size, white rectangles with black, square windows. Dark, dusty alleys separated the buildings, and lines of brightly colored clothes flapped like flags on clotheslines stretched across the rooftops. The city was so simple and straightforward it could almost have been built by a child. That first evening I stood on the roof and watched donkeys with barrels strapped to their sides stopping at doorways to deliver water.

A simple routine emerged. Daytime was a torture chamber, made nearly unbearable by the equatorial heat; nighttime, with its balmy, languid breezes and dinner on lantern-lit patios outside cafes, was simply paradise among the flowering vines. By day, on jeep excursions out to eerie dunes, to the edge of the ocean, where we would plunge into the breakers on beaches of nearly unfathomable solitude, or simply when I crossed the town, darting from shadow to shadow, to do a traveler's business at the bank, the sun bleached away my recent past and with it the craving to write.

The American boys, Peace Corp volunteers, were young princes of the city. Four shared a gigantic empty house, nearly a mansion, with grounds enclosed by a thick adobe fence and swept clean by a big stick broom. Amazingly they had a stereo and a huge library of Delta blues records.

The intent, detailed songs of Lightnin' Hopkins drifted out of that huge, empty house and floated into the maze where stores, like stages, stood open to the alleyways.

The room had little furniture, mostly mattresses on the floor covered with the cheap Madras bedspreads that were ubiquitous in student lodgings everywhere, from Berkeley to Istanbul. Thick candles littered with burnt matches and marijuana roaches stood on the floor in every room, but in the main room—three mattresses there—where the Americans collected around the stereo was a harem: five of the most beautiful women, the most incredibly beautiful women, I had ever seen.

They were half-castes, somebody told me, the children of Italian colonists and the tall, black-skinned Semitic Somali women. And not only half-castes but outcasts—these young girls were prostitutes, almost a third sex next to the law-abiding Moslem men and the women, so heavily veiled in black that they even wore black scarves thrown over their faces. Presumably the women, gliding tents, could see out through the dark chiffon, but you saw nothing at all, not even eyes, except a mound of black—that is, if you dared to look. The prohibition against looking at the women was palpable, but I could literally feel their own judging glances scald my knees.

I was thrilled, though, at the sight of these slender, tan-skinned, blue-eyed women propped up against the white walls in their looping clothes. They wore long, sarong-type skirts and simple blouses in pale flower colors. They were so fine-boned and delicate that the cans of beer they sipped profaned their hands. The American boys seemed bonded together in an impenetrable fraternity, and I had found no way to reach any women of the town. Two American women I had met in the rooftop restaurant where we ate breakfast had hunkered down over their massive omelets and emanated ill humor. But the sight of these wondrous princesses of mixed blood made my traveler's loneliness lift and fade. Outcasts and prostitutes? All the more encouraging to my hope of making human contact out there, where my own spirit had been tossed, beyond the pale.

I seated myself on a mattress near two of the women, smiled, and stretched out my hand to them. I wasn't sure whether or not they spoke English. They turned to look at me in the cool, neutral way gazelles will gaze at a potential invader that has yet to become an active threat. My hand, stretched out in greeting, they ignored. With a hopeful lift of the brows, I pointed to a beer in one of the women's hands. The magnificent eyes, greenish blue against skin of coffee with cream, gazed at me, then past me, then scrutinized the wall. With scarlet-tipped fingers, the beauty closest to me flicked my hand away in irritation and turned her back. No beer for me, and certainly no womanly comfort here. The two girls passed a joint back and forth and, stung, I listened to Lightnin' Hopkins sing on and on about trouble in mind.

From Somalia we flew to Kenya to travel by hitchhiking or rented car from one wildlife preserve to another. And I think it was through the animals, the mere presence of the animals, that I found my way back to the living.

Not that I wasn't afraid. Up to now, entering the wilderness to me had meant going on an overnight with your age group at camp and eating s'mores around the campfire. Simply riding into the endless East African savanna, crawling upward through a bamboo forest on a red mountain road high above the terraced fields of a smoky village, inching through a jungle pierced by the primeval cries of nocturnal hyrax, descending into the bowl of an ancient volcano—all these tightened my stomach with a stunned perception of the hugeness of the world.

But drive for four hours and then stop. Don't speak. Step out of the car and let the sound of the engine fade from your ears. Let the primitive anxiety of a girl from the suburbs gradually sink away. And before you begin to scan the landscape for signs of the creatures inhabiting or just passing through this land, look up and take inventory of the weathers sharing the ocean of sky. Like a fleet of great ships, large clouds near the horizon may be gathering into a storm. Far across the plains is evidence of another. In the rainy season, perhaps five, perhaps six, perhaps ten towering sheets of rain are in view, while sailing above you, and only for a fraction of a second muting the fierce rays of the sun, are small, isolated clouds throwing their moving shadows on the grasses.

Only by degrees can you melt into the landscape. Your eyes need time to forget the motion of the road and learn to search the still expanses for a telltale sign. But then, quite suddenly, to see a few fine-drawn lines resolve into a herd of giraffe grazing on the high branches of a sausage tree! To watch them, for as long as you can see them, stride away and then *gallop*—gigantic stick figures rocking against the horizon like a junkie's dream. Or to discover, with a sense of hilarious *right*ness, that warthogs graze on their knees, and their young, following their mothers through the tall yellow grass, raise their tails straight up so that, though the babies are too small to be seen, flags of hair on the ends of their tails remain visible above the blades!

Drivers who had picked us up were always stopping suddenly and diving for their cameras—and in that way, in a minibus full of irritable flight attendants, I saw a cheetah curled up in a tree. But hitchhiking, you can't always choose your company, and this particular driver suddenly gunned the engine and chased the beast down to make it run. The terrified animal bounded from the branch and disappeared in an instant, before the driver could even snatch the lens cap off his camera.

Gazelle, zebra, wildebeest, ibex, water buck—grazing animals intermingled in their hundreds, and near a water hole you could study their markings for as long as you liked. Sometimes, in the stillness, the only hint that these were real beings was the gamy smell on the hot buzzing air.

We saw a hippo pool containing fat beauties swimming with their babies, as nuttily graceful as any Disney ballerina and far less believable. And we awoke one night on the dusty ground to stare up into the dark universe and listen, with exquisite alertness, to the unmistakable sounds of massive teeth grinding—hippos stepping lightly and feeding in the cool darkness.

Very rarely we heard lions roar in the night, the sounds like great hollow balls thrown out at the sky and rolling at us from far away. And we saw lions in circles by day blinking slowly, sated, of a size and a range of biscuity hues never perceptible in any zoo. But the elephants were what drew me. Their bodies seemed to reflect some cockamamie scheme that just barely worked, the last brainstorm of a genius going off the deep end. In the herds we came across plodding through the bush, standing by a water hole, or sometimes disappearing, running, around the base of a low hill, the complexity of their relationships seemed apparent. With a language of body and eye, they strung themselves together into a loosely connected but clearly defined group.

Back home in Berkeley, walking into the wrong place at the wrong time, being the random target of rageful crazies, had triggered a shortness of vision in me that had made my inner world a nearly suffocating box. The Boyfriend was not the one to shine light into my little protective cave. Perhaps nobody was. But under the pounding equatorial sun, with the visible distances so vast in every direction that the very curve of the earth was revealed, the swish of a tail, the heavy thud of a foot, the quiver of a velvety upper lip, slowly eroded my inner walls. Gradually I was soothed, healed, by the presence of animals. Soon I would be able to lift my eyes, look outward, and begin to cross the nearly impenetrable borders into other people's stories.

There was a day in Kenya when the car in which the Boyfriend and I had hitched a ride across the savanna broke down and the driver and his passenger hiked off down the road to find help. We sat near the car for a full day—not long by East African standards in such matters, but a substantial island of time for us. We sat on a knoll and threw down our packs. Immediately my friend, after checking for snakes, stretched out, placed his hat over his eyes, and let the Kenyan equivalents of cicadas put him to sleep with their high-pitched whine. I took out a book and read.

Half an hour or so later, I looked up to see two Masai boys, one perhaps twelve or thirteen, one seven or eight, standing nearby and staring at us intently. Unlike the village children along the roads who waved at cars but, at our approach on foot, withdrew and stared, these boys watched us unblinking and seemed unfazed by my return stare. I nodded and smiled; they nodded. They seemed content simply to watch us, and I was struck not by the surface differences between us, but by the more profound and subtle ones—about time, for instance, and the conventions of courtesy. After thirty seconds or so, I found I had to drop my gaze. The boys just stared and stared.

"*Jambo,*" I said, offering the Swahili greeting in my ignorance of the Masai word.

"*Jambo,*" the older boy replied. He was tall and skinny as a stick and wore a brown sarong fastened in classic Masai fashion at the shoulder. The smaller boy was dressed in shorts, but both had on beadwork—armbands and necklaces—composed of tiny spots of bright, primary colors.

They stood and stared; I sat and squinted out across the dry, yellow plain. My companion slept on beneath his hat.

Finally I glanced back and smiled and the boys stepped closer, frankly fascinated with the backpacks we had thrown down in relief. "Mmm," said the older one, with an upward gesture of the chin. The littler boy spoke rapidly. "Mmmm," replied the older boy and stepped near.

Over the course of half an hour, we performed a minuet of tiny moves and gestures, and at last they bent their long skinny shiny brown legs and sat down close to the packs.

By infinitesimal degrees, a ritual of discovery ensued. I handed over my book and my elaborate purse for inspection. I showed them how to look through the camera and took their pictures (alas, lost now), and then—to enthusiastic "mms"—I began to unpack my backpack. There was a little wooden flute in there. I tootled on it and passed it around. I had a beautiful scarf and complicated sandals that crossed and recrossed up the leg. These I demonstrated to the older boy, while the little one examined my walking boots.

Together they turned the pages of my journal, and then looked up at me questioningly—no pictures? I had a little traveler's kit full of clever implements—a fold-up scissors, a multibladed knife with an ivory toothpick, a fork and knife for eating, a sewing kit, a small mirror, I forget what else, all carefully fitted into their own compartments. This occupied us for many minutes, and then, repacked, went into the dry grass between us. I laid out a packet of picture postcards I had been adding to from the museums I had visited throughout Europe, and these were studied minutely, slowly, as well appreciated as they could be. Finally I had no more to show, and together we surveyed my belongings in the grass. Then the two divested themselves of their beadwork, or at least of the beadwork that came off easily—some was knotted on with thongs. They laid their things in the circle too, and we sat smiling a bit crazily at one another. They seemed content to sit with me in silence.

In response to some invisible signal that must have passed between us, I began to pack up my things and the boys took up their beads. Then they unfolded like flamingos, smiled broadly down at me still on the ground—I can still recall the dust on their slender cheeks—and departed. They walked into the Kenyan landscape as I had seen many Africans do—simply stepping into the bush toward a destination that was not only invisible to me, but unimaginable as well.

We made our way to a guest house in Uganda near the Mountains of the Moon, a small house set in place within a poinsettia garden. The inn was famous in the literature of the mountain gorilla, and we were hoping for the chance to meet Diane Fossey, the naturalist who would eventually pay with her life for her fierce devotion to preserving the gorillas. But Fossey was back in the States having her teeth seen to—and twenty-three years later I was thrilled to read of that very dental visit in Farley Mowat's riveting biography, *Woman in the Mist.* Walter Baumgartel had run his guest house in Uganda for decades, but now he was calling it quits: "Africanization," he snorted in disgust, would be the ruin of Africa.

Traveling as we were, there was never much chance for solitude, so on a day when my friend went climbing in the Virunga volcanoes in the rain, I stayed behind at the guest house. He had left with a small party at dawn; by breakfast time the wide green lawn and luxuriant poinsettia border that surrounded the house were steaming in the sun.

I was breakfasting alone in a screened sunporch with a book balanced on the salt shaker. Behind me the screen door burst suddenly inward and banged on the screened wall behind it.

"So you serve this lady eggs!" came a deep shout behind me, unmistakably angry.

It was an army officer, impeccable in his uniform. He resembled Idi Amin, who would come into power several years later.

Walter Baumgartel emerged from an interior room. "I am running a business," he retorted, his German accent lending a chiseled effect to the words. "The guests must have eggs."

"The guests must have eggs, but my men, no!" shouted the officer. It was clear that these two had shouted at each other before, and no understanding had been reached. The day had only begun; I knew Baumgartel had had no argument that morning, because I'd awakened to see my friend off. But over my head these two launched into a full confrontation without even working up to it—they were clearly picking up where they had last left off.

My eggs, in grease that tasted much like soapsuds, lay innocently upon my plate, two unblinking eyes. I stared at them and hoped to dissolve as the shouting match proceeded. Disgust crept into Baumgartel's voice. "How must I run a business if I give the army all my eggs? You tell me that, must I give you all my eggs? It's fourteen men, what's that, twenty-eight, forty-two eggs every morning? Nearly four dozen eggs. Am I to donate this amount to the army of Uganda every morning before I feed my guests?" He was becoming shrill.

"I have little concern for your business. You and your guests and your business can go to hell."

And so they stared at each other above my head, and I felt their mutual hatred as if it were an electrical current. I had seen the gun in the elaborate leather holster the officer wore on his khaki uniform, and I fervently prayed to the eggs that he would cool down and go away.

The moment stretched on, and finally I had to turn and look at the man at my back—it seemed offensive not to, and I certainly wished to give no offense to either of them at that moment. I looked at the officer, beautifully turned out in his khaki, leather, and lovely white trim, and he drilled me with his eyes for another interminable moment before turning on his heels and leaving.

Baumgartel clucked to himself like a hen and busied himself with his newspaper, standing at the kitchen door. "You see how it is, you see how it is. Twenty-five years I have lived here, made this place. Made this place a world center for students of the mountain gorilla—yes, yes, you can read about it in many books, I have put this place on the map. And then they give it to them, they simply *give* it to them. You put them into a uniform and that's the end of it. You see how it is, you see how it is, young lady. Well, I shall not have to put up with it much longer—every day this one comes in to bother my guests. You see how it is and why I must pack up my things and leave."

The incident remained in my mind just as it had happened, as if it had been a play staged for maximum effect. I think it possible that if the anger had heated by another degree or two I might have become a casualty to the racial hatred blanketing the globe.

Baumgartel rattled his paper and, reading, wandered away. I eyed my eggs and thought them shiny, soggy mementos of what was my instant of sharpest reality in Africa. Just for the morning, the maddening, invisible bunting that keeps travelers from experiencing the real life of the places they pass through had been pierced by the hatred that fuels murder, rape, even war.

Now that the walls were down, I began to see: it was a question of surviving your raw material. Whatever life offered, and *only* what it offered, would become the stuff of art. The challenge was to live through it and then look back open-eyed without flinching. It occurred to me then that if I ever picked up my pad and pencil again, I might actually have some stories to tell.

FOUR

Borders

It was in Israel that I began to come up hardest against the borders of understanding, learning a difficult lesson about the limits of empathy in the face of profound cultural divisions. It was unusually cold and wet throughout the Middle East that winter, and my companion and I decided to wait out the weather by volunteering on a kibbutz in exchange for food and shelter.

To my surprise, in the group of thirty or so volunteers on our kibbutz, I was one of very few Jews. It was Christmas time when we joined the group and, endearingly, the kibbutzniks took an interest in how these thirty or so *goyishe* travelers would celebrate their exotic Christian ritual. They brought in a freshly killed turkey and even secured a case of canned cranberries—an embarrassment of cranberries—for the occasion. And they supplied three trucks with benches in the back to haul us to Jerusalem. The trucks dropped us off at 11 P.M., in time for midnight mass.

Hokey light shows were the rage at cultural sites world-wide, but in the courtyard of the ancient church in the heart of Jerusalem, the effect was less tacky than bizarre. The lights on the stone walls threw into eerie relief the figures of soldiers pacing the rooftops surrounding the square. Everywhere rifle-bearing soldiers were outlined against the sky, adding a defiant spin to the Christmas spirit in that ancient setting. We strolled below like the inhabitants of a guarded fort.

The Boyfriend had stayed behind. My friends were two Australian longhairs, Miles and Randy, and Max, from London, who shaved his head and was as canny and jaded as a New York City cabbie. Separately and in various combinations, the three had been on the road for years—six years, in Max's case, moving from job to job ahead of the weather. They had come to Israel from Greece, and their motivation for moving on seemed to be a blend of boredom and marijuana. For the time being, the cold-water volunteer lodgings and communal showers at the kibbutz seemed to suit them fine. In Jerusalem we passed on going to mass and bought a bottle of *arak,* the anise-based liquor that tasted deceptively like licorice candy. Then we strolled through the dark alleyways to a restaurant they knew.

Arab stores were shut up tight, the corrugated pull-down doors breaking up the stone facades. Second-floor windows lit our way, and I strove in vain for glimpses of the family life going on just above our heads. Here and there a wrapped figure passed us in the dark, and I remember the atmosphere now as more in keeping with the foggy London nights of *Dr. Jekyll and Mr. Hyde* than the sultry night-time promises of *The Arabian Nights*. Rain threatened and in patches actually fell, the promised restaurant seemed only a remote rumor, and all but Max had given up hope of finding it by the time we followed him down steps into a dark cavern of a place and were led by a waiter through a low-ceilinged maze. We were ushered into our own little nook, and Max brought out another bottle of *arak*—forbidden by religious and civil law, too, I think—from under his biker jacket.

We ate pilaf and many kinds of relishes and unnamed delicacies—all exotic, some sweet to my taste, others vinegary and acrid. Textures, too, eluded me. What *were* these foods—meats, fruits, berrylike things as condiments to the pilaf? Perhaps these last were raisins, but I didn't think so. Food kept coming, the talk grew more raucous, and the *arak* was passed in a brown paper bag.

"Sir," someone said from the door—a young Palestinian man of about twenty-five, the approximate age of us all.

"Yes, yes, come in. Don't hang about by the door, come in, come in," shouted Max, quite drunk by now and spitting when he talked.

"Sir," said the man, "may we come into please?"

"Come in, come in, for God's sake," yelled Max.

"To practice Anglish? It is students."

"Oh, yes, of course, but get on with it, won't you?" Max had an impatience to match, tie, and wallop that of the Israelis any day. He was a brilliant boy in whom the experiences of life evoked equal parts disgust and lugubrious sentiment. He often wore a grimace on his face, and it was difficult to decide as you talked to him whether he was sympathizing painfully with what you said or about to take you out with a barbed insult.

"Okay, okay, but my friends," said the young man at the door. He turned away and then back, and four more young Palestinian men filed into the close little cave of a room. All wore white dress shirts with starched open collars. Their black hair was highlighted in the low lamplight; their dark brows conveyed earnest courtesy. Each carried his dinner plate and a side or relish dish from his own table. "This is your holy day?" asked one dazzling young fellow, his eyes under shapely brows picking up the candlelight.

"Our holy day? Oh, yes, yes. Christmas."

"The birthday of your Christ?"

"Yes, the birthday of our Christ."

"So. You say, happy birthday, no?"

Max brought out the paper bag containing the *arak*. "Well, happy birthday, then," he told them. They greeted the sight of the bottle with syllables of muted enthusiasm, and the liquor made the circle. By this time I was quietly, if not quite leadenly, drunk. As the party gained steam, I let the bottle pass.

Twice more the bottle made the rounds of the table, and then Miles asked one of our visitors, "Could I taste that perhaps? Just a bite to taste?" Thus began a complex sharing of food that amounted to a lesson in Palestinian cuisine. Plates were passed across the table, forkfuls of food were handed around, combinations of relishes had to be sampled and remarked upon. With nine young men passing plates and forks, the table took on the complexity of a piece of Arabic calligraphy, and as the noise level rose, I became infected with the cross-cultural spirit.

"Could I try some?" I asked a fellow across from me, and his cohorts fell suddenly silent. In another second the five of them had risen, taken their plates, and filed out of the room, leaving a trail of outrage like an odor. The four of us were left to stare at each other, dumbstruck.

After a second Max pulled out of it. "You sure know how to throw a party, Sue."

"But—" I protested, hoping there was some explanation other than the fact than I had spoken up and asked to share the food.

"Welcome to the Middle East," said Randy. "Didn't you know they were just barely tolerating your presence at the table?"

"No, I certainly did *not* know that."

"These were modern guys, used to Western ways and Western women, but the idea of sharing food with you was just too much. When you pointed your fork at that one guy's food, he just grabbed his plate and ran."

"You mean they were disgusted?" I asked, humiliated.

"Disgusted? I don't know. More like shocked."

We paid and left, and as we filed past the students' table, the five young men kept their eyes riveted to their plates.

"It's the movies," said Max. "American movies play everywhere in the world, and everywhere in the world American women come off like whores. Try watching *Valley of the Dolls* through Eastern eyes sometime. These guys probably thought they'd get stoned on amphetamines if they let you taste their pilaf."

"Or gonorrhea," said Miles.

I felt awful—embarrassed and awkward, wronged and mortified. Perhaps I *was* too forward, maybe I was even disgusting. It was true I was tall and blond, not at all like the small mounds under dark purdah cloaks, the women of the Old Town, who seemed to glide rather than walk through the alleyways. I fell asleep in the truck with the boys that night torn between their delicious company and the distinct feeling that the impressions of the world I was collecting and sketching so lovingly in my travel journal were coming to me through a narrow tube.

My trip would yield many ideas, many details, that would find their way into stories, but perhaps none so mysterious and ultimately so fruitful as my growing sense that reality was a mosaic. That one event—a simple meal shared with students—could appear so wildly different to observers at the same table was a writer's lesson worth the face-reddening embarrassment with which I left the restaurant. Not writing alone, not even writing with empathy, makes a writer. It is writing plus *life* that makes a writer . . . because life alone creates a point of view. Irony of ironies, the more separations we experience, one from another, the more stories we have to tell—and the more pressing becomes the need to tell them.

FIVE

A Healing

A Turkish vessel, the *Iskenderun,* made the hippie run from Haifa to Istanbul. Third-class passage was amazingly cheap—six or seven American dollars, I think. By day, for the three-day voyage, third-class passengers stayed in a large, comfortable, if crowded salon. I found it rather cozy, a great relief after the hard work of the winter on the kibbutz, to curl up and read for whole days at a stretch. I read books discarded by other volunteers that I'd picked up at the kibbutz with a constant feeling of good luck at having found them. There were long, languid, information-exchanging conversations with others doing the route and not bad meals. The wooden benches in the salon were shiny and smooth and golden. Intermittently rain spattered the windows that closed off the salon from the third-class deck. And sometimes when the fog lifted we saw islands furred with evergreen trees.

At night the third-class passengers slept in dorms in the very bowels of the ship next to the engines. We glided through cool, gray days on a calm sea, but the nights were a hell of thumping heat and noise. There were six women in my dorm, stacked up in three bunk beds.

At night the crew wandered.

I wrote a poem about that first night, wakening, in the bowels of the *Iskenderun*.

> Midnight shadows, human rats,
> Wake with the roll of the waves.
> One leaves the pack,
> Stirred by a dream
> To a taste for flesh.
> Bending into a scuttle
> Through the metal corridors
> He moves,
> But the scratching of his claws
> Is muffled
> By the creak and whine
> Of the ship.
>
> Three times below deck
> He pauses,
> Ears twitching,
> At an open door.
> The horrid sharp nose
> Lusts for moist bodies,
> The tiny cruel teeth
> Clench nervously
> At the sound of a
> Rustling sheet.

Six female creatures
Are stacked in a two-fold row
And pressed heavily into sleep
By the stifling air.
The man-rat, hungry night rat,
Waters with the hunger of
Unfinished dreams.
He darts silently inside
And buries his face in flesh.
He draws hard and deep
At the ancient smell.

Hunched on the altar,
Low in his throat,
He makes a growling prayer.

I woke up with a yell that was lost in the pounding of
the engines, and waving my beloved hairbrush, token of
home, chased that morbid creature through the narrow
corridors of metal. But he knew the ship and darted aside
into some secret passageway, leaving me standing alone
under a naked light bulb trailing a sweaty sheet.

It is twenty-two years since that sickening hour rushing
through dark waters, and I'm still grateful for the impulse I
had to cast it into the words of a poem and fling it back
into the universe. And yet I was left with a terrible loneliness, an illness of the soul. This was *too much*—traveling
the world and soaking up life were innocent efforts, harm-
less. No poem, no journal, no exercise in point of view, not
the most sincere desire to cross the boundaries of personal

history or culture would ever protect against the dangers of the real, physical world. I was twenty-five and beaten down. My womanhood was greatly at risk.

Istanbul, golden apple of the Ottoman empire, was bleak and freezing, and clumps of unemployed men, all wearing caps that seemed straight out of the Great Depression, stood on street corners and smoked. We stayed in a hippie hotel that turned out to have no hot water. Typed warnings of long prison terms for drug possession, written by other young travelers, were taped to the walls of the corridors and gloomy rooms.

We were dirty and freezing, and I had not bathed in the two days since that terrible night aboard ship. Following directions spelled out in my notebook by a hitchhiker in Uganda, we made our way to a *hamam* in the city center. On our way through the city, we passed the Hagia Sofia mosque looming in all its complexity against the leaden sky.

My companion left to bathe in the men's public baths. I entered the women's section, never suspecting that in crossing the threshold I was once more stepping far back in time. The reception area was small and nondescript; a woman behind the counter took the fee and handed me a towel and wooden bath sandals. With her chin she pointed me through a white curtain, behind which I found a double door. Pushing through, I entered a corridor of cubicles, where I undressed and left my clothes.

At the end of the hall was another set of double doors, and behind these I found myself in a gigantic, resounding, domed room filled with clouds of steam. As I stood just inside the door, still braced against the Turkish winter chill, the thick, moist heat swirled around me, licked and encoiled me. The heat drew me in and embraced me, and seeing the naked women flashing and shining everywhere, I clutched my towel to myself and stepped into an echoing secret world. Gray sky filtered in through the misted ornamental windows of the dome, and all colors below were muted by the steam. The vast circle was banded by two marble steps to be used as benches, and at intervals around the room, steady streams of steaming water fell into marble basins. Gathered round these basins and immersed in the hot waters of a rectangular common pool were naked women of every description—from babies and little girls to old, old, drooping women, from singular beauties to staunch peasanty bodies in their middle years. All stripped of their clothes, they lacked the markers that would have hinted at who they were, where they fit into the social order, how they spent their time. These women were naked strangers offering no physical clues to their identities other than the signs of age they could not hide. If any drug vision had ever moved and fascinated me, it paled in comparison to this ring of languid women.

Self-conscious, I held my towel to my chest and let it drape over my body as I searched for a spot near one of the basins. I found one close by and sat down on my towel, giving myself over to the warm mist and relinquishing my

modesty as my body, which had been shivering for days—
in disgust at the shipboard incident as well as from the bitter late-winter cold—turned slowly to a soft dough and
melted over the shiny marble ledge.

In the middle of the room was a huge marble slab, and
there old naked women—their black hair in long, damp
strings, their mouths open with their efforts, revealing
gaps from lost teeth—worked over white, rounded figures
stretched out full length on the stone platform. Some of
the crones massaged with the full weight of their bodies,
and the muscles in their arms flashed here and there through
veils of swinging flesh. Others rubbed or gently whipped
the bodies they worked upon with bundles of black twigs.
The old women exchanged occasional remarks over the
women beneath their hands, and by some acoustical oddity
their words sliced through the ringing noise of running
water in sharp streaks of sound.

All around me women groomed themselves from the
bottles and soaps they had brought with them. Never
imagining a scene so timeless, I had brought nothing. As I
began to splash warm water artlessly over my shoulders
with a cupped hand, I felt an old woman approach me
from the center. She stood before me in her raised, wooden
sandals—you can see versions of the same sandals, called
pattens, in old engravings of the baths. She was very old,
probably in her late seventies, if my Western standards applied, and the force of gravity was apparent on her thighs,
her breasts, her belly in sections, all lined and cross-lined
with tiny wrinkles. Down her center was an old scar, twelve

inches vertical, cutting through the rolls of fat to the shiny, hairless mound. The sight of her nudity made me shy. She smiled a creased smile and beckoned to me, then pointed to the marble slab, and I followed her like a well-mannered child.

She spread my towel for me and laid me down, and I rested the pad of my cheek against the towel and allowed her to pull my hands out to my sides until I lay spread-eagle on my corner of the slab. I willed myself to receive without flinching the touch of her bony hands on my back. But the hands were those of a nurse or a baker—strong, young-seeming hands, sure and warm, the palms and thumbs together delivering health and deep relaxation in the form of direct, perpendicular pressure.

The old woman shaped me as if I were a loaf of dough or a long, dense log of clay. She worked down my backbone with the heels of her hands, stretching her fingers across the back of my ribs. She kneaded my buttocks with short, pinchlike strokes. She worked down the backs of my thighs with efficiency, never missing an inch. From months of carrying a backpack by the sides of roads—highways, city streets, the red dirt roads of East Africa, the ribbons of shimmering blacktop through the Negev Desert—my shoulders and calves were stubborn knots; she returned to them again and again with tough, insistent fingers.

When she had molded my body to the shape that satisfied her, the old woman took up a bundle of the mysterious black twigs and tapped it over every inch of my skin. Then she made another pass, lightly brushing, and yet another, tapping with a somewhat circular motion. Almost gone, my mind nearly merged with the swirling mist rising to the dome above me, I felt the heavy weight of hot, wet towels laid end to end along my body.

I was clean, inside and out. There was little left in me but gratitude to the woman whose hands had taken their time to stroke and knead me. I was clean and warm, a child in the hands of an old, knowing woman whose very body spoke survival of her own nameless ordeals. To have come to this place of women and fallen into her hands was a life-saving accident, and though we never spoke and I never knew her name—and in fact she left me before I roused myself and I did not see her again—I think that old woman saved me for the rest of my journey. Perhaps it didn't matter that she never could have known. And yet perhaps she *had* known—perhaps she had, for the dangers to women everywhere were then and are still very great—that she helped me step back into myself.

My friend and I had already visited many countries and dipped into or skimmed many different cultures. But so rarely had I managed to cross the *real* borders between the people I met and myself that I had nearly given up. In my profound distress, without my even realizing it, my understanding of others had all but drained away, leaving me bewildered and adrift, even in the closest company.

It was not until I walked back out into the city, the cold and noise penetrating the muzzy film the warmth and wet had wrapped around my mind, that I had even the slightest idea that I had been outside my body for a long, long time.

My friend and I stopped for orange juice at a stand on the edge of the traffic, and I drank two. Dehydrated and famished, I tapped with my finger at the bottom of the paper cup to dislodge the orange pulp. With my tongue I popped the clusters of flavorful morsels against the roof of my mouth—and for me the gray winter world filled with color and all the people in the streets suddenly snapped alive.

CULTIVATING

SIX

Mad Cassandra

Finally the frail tendrils between the Boyfriend and me tore, and we parted ways. I simply headed east, choosing my stopping places almost randomly. I took the train across Turkey, riding backwards nearly all the way. The trip took four days; I was the sole woman in a compartment with four men. On the day we left Istanbul, I ate something in a small station, sold by a vendor through the window of our car. The men watched me while I made the transaction, and it became a matter of pride to finish the stuff—a meat in red sauce of such an exotic consistency I couldn't identify it even as to species of beast. Within minutes my belly had swelled, and at first with discretion, later in desperation, I unbuttoned the waistband of my jeans and inched the zipper down under my shirt. For four days I suffered as we crossed Turkey in our little wheeled box.

It was yet another country where the women were hidden away. Or did they hide themselves? For a generation the women of Turkey had been unveiled by decree, stripped of the dark, swirling purdah wraps that had kept them secret and mysterious even within their own households.

Now, exposed to the eyes of the men and of each other, they still managed to obliterate themselves and together to seem like a people apart. Many, of all ages, wore black and covered their legs with peach-colored hose thick as bandages. Their hair, braided and pinned, they covered with black babushkas. From the train window, as we chugged through the Turkish countryside, I watched armies of women dressed this way, shopping tirelessly. I hadn't the imagination to penetrate their anonymity.

In Istanbul I had seen young, modern women moving quickly here and there through the sea of black shadows. These bold young women stood out in sharp relief. Their courage made them even more exotic than the others. To expose an inch of leg above a tall boot, to wear the hair cut short with a businesslike sweep across the brow: each line of their bodies was a challenge and a defiance.

Throughout the city the women intermingled in a strange dance, whispering to each other behind their hands and struggling, it seemed, across the centuries, to make contact. Dark women of the old style moved slowly in groups through the streets; penetrating the mass of black rushed the young modern women: like atoms, propelled from within and without.

The men stood in clumps, smoking darkly. The dance of the women went on around them, and they turned the tension of it onto young female travelers, transients, like me. They jeered at us, hearty American, European, Australian girls as innocent and stupid as calves. The men watched us approaching and clacked their tongues against the roofs of their mouths in a wet imitation of sex. The insult was so savage we sometimes missed the point and smiled back in idiotic friendliness. They scratched their genitals. Some exposed themselves with a quick motion: Did it happen? we asked ourselves in fright.

No other women were apparent in my car on the train carrying me away from that deranged city. All the compartments were filled with men, their wool caps lined up on the luggage racks along with their bulky packages, tied together with belts. The men on the train were kinder than those on the streets of the city. I rode along with them, fidgeting with my clothes. At night they unhinged the wooden shelves that served as beds, and I crawled onto a top bunk. All through the night, as I rolled with the distress of mild food poisoning and the anxiety that it might burgeon into a full-blown case, the glowing tips of cigarettes pierced the compartment's darkness.

We didn't speak to each other or even try after the first few hours. We did nod; they accepted my presence as part of their own journey, but they slid sidelong glances at me as I read. I felt they stared at me when I finally managed to sleep.

But the sound of the train wheels muted everything: the men's talk, our curiosity about each other, the passing of time itself. The four days on the train formed a small patch of reality apart, within which the five of us sat, gazing out the window at the gray Turkish landscape and the beautiful lines of black, leafless trees.

On the fourth day, I strolled the length of the train for perhaps the hundredth time, peering into compartment after compartment without thinking, as if riffling through postcards.

"Come off it, Cass, you fucking cunt."

The man's voice was raised with such fury it rang out over the racket of the wheels.

Trying to appear casual, I dared to look in, my hunger for English whetted.

I could only see a woman—slender, dark, about thirty-five. She lounged on the seat facing me, one foot up on the velveteen upholstery, an arm flung across her knee. Her head was tipped back and her face composed into a viciously sarcastic smile: open-mouthed, teeth flashing, accepting the challenge of the words I had heard.

She was tiny, and confidently American. She wore white gauze pants and delicate sandals, and her long shirt was made of light Indian cotton subtly striped with silver threads. What was riveting, as she casually brought her other arm around behind her head, were the small dark nipples, like olives, that flashed beneath the cloth of her see-through shirt.

The furious words I'd heard and the days of being walled in by the impenetrable sounds of Turkish had made me reticent, but the desire to exchange words without effort actually wet my tongue. When I'd gone the length of the train I strolled back with a resolve to stand by the open compartment and introduce myself. But the door was shut; I wasn't even sure which one it had been.

The next step on my route was to be Ezurum, a town on the border between Turkey and Iran. As was usual on a long segment of my journey, the destination during the four days on the train had grown infinitely desirable in my mind: I pictured a fantasy city of spires and movie houses, sidewalk cafes and mosaicked hotels. In reality I found Ezurum a disordered mess of quonset huts and unpaved, red-dust roads. On the facade of nearly every building, residential or commercial, was a paint-peeled, rusted Coca-Cola or Pepsi advertising plaque, and all the doors were shut tight—all rolled corrugated metal, pulled down firmly and locked.

I stood on the platform watching the train pull away and felt furious and bereft at having been betrayed by my own innocence. I had come on this trip to gain a sense of motion, of change, but here all was still. From where I stood, I could see the boundaries of the town in all directions.

The American woman I had seen on the train stood some yards from me, digging for matches in a huge string bag, a cigarette dangling from her lips. She could have been standing by the subway tracks below New York City for all the interest she took in her surroundings. Her main concern in life seemed to be finding a light. Behind her was a tall man of about thirty, seemingly younger than her by five or six years. His face was so lovely the word *handsome* was entirely inadequate. The shape itself, the play of fine muscle into expression, was fascinating. The man was looking past the town, squinting slightly toward the harsh yellow mountains to the north.

"Shit," he breathed with obvious disgust.

"Hey, why don't you relax for a change, Michael?" said the woman, Bogart-fashion, around the cigarette. Her voice was the nasal whine of a Brooklyn street kid. She continued to dig in her bag.

"Hey, just shut up, Cass. Okay?" he spat at her, and abruptly walked to the end of the platform to a bench against the wall of the station hut. He collapsed there, beaming irritation and boredom at the red, treeless foothills.

She took no notice, found a match, and lit her cigarette with a deep draw.

A man wearing a wool cap came out of the station house and approached her. "Hotel, shhvvtt," he shouted, trying to overcome the language barrier by sheer volume. "What?" she asked, looking up, and I drew closer. "Hotl, hotl, shhvvtt," and he pointed to the book of matches in her hand. Again he said, "Shhvvtt, shhvvtt," and made a frantic horizontal gesture with his hands.

"Oh, great," she said, looking my way for the first time but hurling her sarcasm at me with complete familiarity. "The hotel burned down. They knew we were coming. Hey, Michael," she shouted—brayed—suddenly, not turning toward him, and I felt her hot breath on my face, "the hotel burned down."

He didn't move.

"Coom, coom," said the man in the wool cap, and he tugged gently at her white, flowing sleeve, which she removed from his grasp with an automatic gesture. "Coom, coom." I suddenly realized he meant "come."

"I think he wants to take us to a place to stay," I said.

"So let's go," and she turned to the pile of luggage behind her. "Hey, Michael," she yelled. "Come on, help me out here, this guy's showing us a place to stay." She turned back to me, shouldering a huge bag of soft, expensive-looking leather. "God, I need a bath," she said.

I introduced myself, feeling absurdly formal.

"Cassandra Burch," she answered flatly. "Let's go. He'll bring the rest." She strode confidently away from the luggage. "I want to take a nice, long, hot, thorough bath."

The man led us down the raw red street that fronted the station. This was clearly the main street, the only paved street, in town. I wondered whether we were being pirated into paying too much for lodgings. But it was clear we had no choice, so we filed along the empty street like lambs.

We stopped in front of a hut identical to the rest, except that it sported a number of soft-drink plaques on its front wall instead of just one, and a dusty Coca-Cola clock whose hands had stuck together at ten past two. The corrugated metal door, almost as wide as the building itself, was halfway up, and a dark cave was revealed, lighted somewhere deep inside by a single bulb. Our guide shouldered the door the rest of the way up and approached a man, apparently the proprietor, who was sitting at a card table and doing accounts in a tall, thin book. Other men sat at similar tables with saucers and tiny demitasse cups piled before them. The central fixture was a pool table, its dark wood gleaming, its green felt spotless. This was the coffee house in my fantasy of an energetic metropolis. Its patrons were hibernating here, hiding from the sunlight that was beginning to pound the dusty town.

I had learned on my travels that at the very worst moments, the moments just this side of despair, someone always stepped up and began to speak English. Suddenly business would be transacted or a decision made, and the motion of the journey, seemingly halted forever in a web of misunderstandings, would resume. In this coffee house, where Cassandra and I sat down at a table at the end of our possibilities, the proprietor welcomed us in English and yelled for a pot of coffee.

Michael came in as if entering an empty room and threw the luggage he was carrying into a pile at Cass's feet. He settled himself at a card table near ours, took out a pocket flask, and set it on the table. He and Cass could have been two strangers on a ship of thousands.

Introductions took place, chiefly between the proprietor and me:

"You know English?" I asked him.

"Yes, a little. You are from . . . ?"

"California."

"Ah," he responded lasciviously, "Cali—*for*—nia."

When the subject of accommodations came up, Michael roused himself and joined with Cass to insist on total privacy for the night.

"But sir," objected the proprietor, "we are no hotel, we have no rooms with beds. You must find comfort here in the cafe. It will be good, I will give you covers. With the fire, it is warm." He indicated the benches built against three walls. Two patrons were currently availing themselves of the benches, though neither was sleeping; both were propped on their elbows, staring at us. Everyone—perhaps fifteen men—was arrested in his ritual of coffee drinking and smoking to stare at us, unblinking.

"Like hell," shouted Michael. "I'm not sleeping on a fucking bench."

"And I need a bath," yelled Cass. Both were continually on the brink of hollering; even in normal conversation, I had noticed, they were primed to demand or insist. The gentle proprietor, trying hard to protect both his dignity and his interests, was no match for them. "I want a bath and a private room to sleep in. We will pay. *We must have these things,*" said Cassandra, spitting out the words, enunciating.

Michael took a long drink from his flask, while the other men in the room eyed him with obvious caution and concern. He was a threat here—everything that came with him into this passed-over town was a threat: the flask, the women, the unreasonable demands. He was a terrible menace in this dark room, and Cassandra and I were dangerous too.

In her stubborn insistence, Cass straightened her back and threw back her shoulders so that her dark nipples pressed against the gauzy white fabric of her shirt.

Anxiously the proprietor capitulated, waving his two open palms in front of his chest in a gesture of conciliation. Perhaps he feared that in another minute Cassandra would assault him with the black nuggets she swung with such alarming aggressiveness just beneath the filmy cloth. There would be no bath, but the private room he could manage. As we would learn, he was giving up his own private quarters, and he too, like Michael, would eschew the benches that lined the wall. Instead he would spend the night curled up on the pool table, with the single blanket he had saved for himself folded under his feet to protect the felt.

The room off the main one didn't represent much of a victory. It was furnished with a large double-sized mattress on the floor and an ugly, dark bureau that seemed distinctly un-Turkish. A variety of carpet scraps made an uneven, multileveled floor covering. Dim light entered a small, unglazed window high up near the ceiling. A naked light bulb dangled down on a wire and a mirror hung from a nail on the door frame. A soft black-and-white snapshot of a young woman in purdah was stuck awry in the frame of the mirror.

We had arrived on the train at eleven in the morning. It couldn't have been more than one o'clock when we were shown to the room. A long day stretched in front of us before we had to face the prospect of sharing the bed on the floor in the cafe proprietor's private room.

I walked the length of the town back and forth as I had walked the length of the train. My feet in open sandals grew dusty; insects buzzed loudly in the awful heat. Was this the extent of daily life one could expect from the town of Ezurum? Did the town come alive at night, perhaps, when the sun had dropped behind the jagged mountains over the Iran border? And where the hell were the women? What claustrophobic rooms in the small thick-walled houses did *they* inhabit? Somehow the day faded into late afternoon, and finally evening shadows crept across the dusty orange road, bringing a chill that would have been unimaginable in the full heat of noon.

We sat inside the cafe with the corrugated door pulled tight. Some men played pool; others watched a patron sketch the Hagia Sofia mosque in colored chalks on a wall of the cafe. Michael watched the picture take on detail and made disparaging remarks loudly to himself as he drank cokes from bottles, his flask emptied hours earlier. Cass dragged book after book from her string bag and paged restlessly through the back issues of *Newsweek* and *Time* that had accumulated there.

We ate greasy kebabs and rice. Finally it grew late enough. The cafe emptied out; several men, travelers like us, lay down on the benches around the walls to sleep.

The three of us faced each other for a moment around the mattress on the floor, and then concerned ourselves with the details as if we'd gone to bed together all our lives. Cassandra and I silently cleared the mattress, relaid the sheet, and smoothed out the thin blankets. I stuffed some clothes in my sweater for a pillow and lay down tentatively, close to the wall. Cass sat on the edge of the bed and smoked, and Michael squatted against the wall, dangling his empty flask on his knee.

"So, Suzanne, here we are," said Cass, with an ironic smile.

I ached to be alone. It had been days and days since I'd been in a room by myself.

"So let's ask the obvious question," she went on, lifting her brows and cocking her head in mock interest. "What brings you to wherever this is?"

"You're right, where *is* this?"

"You got me. Couldn't read it. You ought to ask your friend the cafe owner tomorrow how you pronounce the name of this dump. He thinks you're quite the thing, I notice. You have that *knack,* I bet, for making friends everywhere you go, am I right?" The last words arched into sarcasm so undisguised I ducked it, pretending she wanted to know.

"No, not at all. I'm shy, really. He just likes me because I said I was from California. People seem to perk up when they hear the word California."

"Well, they should," she returned conversationally, "since California is the cunt of the world. Right, Michael?" she shouted at him as if to wake him up. "California's the cunt of the world, right, Mike?"

"Hey, *you're* the cunt of the world," he muttered heavily into his knees. I saw he was stoned out of his mind.

"Oh, real nice, *real* nice." She turned back to me and smiled. "Nice talk from my honey, right? Don't be offended. He's really a wonderful person inside. Trouble is, it's the outside that shows. But he's so beautiful I have to forgive him. Look how beautiful he is. Don't you think he's gorgeous?"

She was daring me to look, unmistakably turning this accidental situation into some sort of territorial battle. Looking back, I see she was making a pathetic display, a flying bird defending her reflection in a glass. But as I lay there, I could feel anger building like heat and I stiffened at the thought of being drawn into their fight. I folded my arms across my eyes and lay still, sensing the plains and mountains of Turkey spreading away from us in the dark. I was trapped in this sad, stark room.

"So. Now. California," she said, using the word like a name and launching her attack. "Tell me why *you're* traveling. No, no, wait, let me guess. Is it because you just adore people and want to learn all you can about our planet's multifarious cultures? Or, no. Wait. Is it because you have a restless nature and just can't bear to stay in one place too long?"

From under my arm I saw her bite at the corner of her lip, staring at the blank wall. The ironic sweetness of her tone rang in the silent room.

"Look, I haven't . . . " I managed.

"No, I've got it," she went on, picking at the thread. "You're from California. *I* know. You're traveling to the East to plumb your spiritual depths, to find a guru and become en*light*ened. Am I right? Am I right? To find the perfect teacher and approach him in the fullest humility, groveling, begging him to take you on as a student? Michael, don't you think that's her reason? She's traveling East with her eyes downcast, hoping to become a richer, deeper, *better* human being?"

"Would you just shut the fuck up, for Christ's sake?"

"You want to know what *I'm* doing in this part of the world?" she asked, pretending we were having a conversation. "Good question. I'm asking myself what I'm doing in this room. . . . If you want to know, it's the clothes." She smirked. "I'm going shopping."

"Look, come on . . . " I objected, floundering, completely out of my depth.

"But travel is so *interesting*," she minced back at me. "Travel is so edu*ca*tional. Let me tell you something, dear," she spat, "people travel because they're bored. Boredom, the universal emotion. People travel because they can't stand sitting night after night staring at the walls, or at their husbands and wives, isn't that so, Michael, darling? Now, Michael here knows all about boredom, because Michael *specializes* in boredom, isn't that right? He *makes* himself as boring as he can blowing pot all day and night."

"Look, Cass," I managed, "things are tough enough here, don't you think? Let's just try to get through this in as friendly a way as we can."

But she was off and running. "Hey, I'll tell *you* something. The last thing I need is some sort of spiel from a jellyfish like you. Okay?"

"Yeah, sure. Okay," I said. I got up and walked out. Whatever form of ostracism I had to face outside from the patrons of the cafe had it all over the ugliness accumulating inside this little room, tremblingly lit to a sickly yellow by a low-watt light bulb on a cord.

Men drank their coffee silently. A young, white-shirted man with a beautiful Omar Sharif mustache shot pool. The periodic click of the balls seemed only to punctuate the words penetrating the unstained plywood door.

"But I was just getting to the part about Michael," she yelled after me. "I thought for sure you'd want to hear all about Michael."

"Hey!" shouted Michael, "Cass! Will you shut the fuck up?" I sat down at a table and smiled what I realized was a totally American smile, heavily weighted with an irony I hoped would separate me from the two behind the door. No luck—all eyes in the place were cast down, and the intentness with which all were listening, despite the language barrier, couldn't have been cracked with a mallet.

"Will you just shut your mouth for a change, you incredible bitch? Hey, and by the way. Don't talk about me as if I'm not in the room, get it? I really mean that. I hate for somebody to talk about me as if I'm not in the goddamn room."

In the silence that followed, something painful was happening—language or no language, I was sure everybody could tell he was hurting her, maybe pinching her arm, and staring her down while he did it.

A tight sound, like the yelp of a kicked dog, electrified us all.

"Now, shut off that goddamn light," he growled, and even that sound, even the little sounds of settling on an unfamiliar mattress, came through the plywood door.

"Caffe?" asked the proprietor, and set a demitasse before me. Grateful for the human interaction, I could only answer with a smile and sip as frugally as possible in defense against certain insomnia from the thick, bitter brew. He stood for a moment looking deep into my eyes, and I remembered the snapshot of the young woman stuck into the frame of the mirror.

"The picture," I said, unsure whether he would understand me. "Is it your wife?"

He stared at me as if down a long road into the sun. And then, "Ah, the photograph! My wife? Yes, yes, not now. Soon. Soon."

"You are going to marry her?"

"Yes, yes, soon. When money."

"You save your money?"

"Yes, my money. For the wife. For my wife I get money. To buy." He grinned broadly.

"I guess it takes a lot of games of pool to buy a wife," I answered, smiling also.

"Pool? Ah, pool?" he smiled and shrugged, and then translated rapidly to the coffee drinkers scattered at their separate tables.

"You are right, lady," said a deep-voiced man. I recognized him as the artist whose half-finished chalk drawing of Hagia Sofia mosque covered the wall behind him. "It takes many pool games to buy a wife." He spoke English confidently, and I ventured a sincere compliment on his art.

"Ach," he said, and waved away the mention. He turned his eyes to the smoke rising from his cigarette. There would be no conversation here.

Oh, God, where were the women? I was dying for want of human contact. Here I was, deep in the heart of another culture, by chance at the social nexus—the coffee-drinking center—of the town, and completely unable to engage anyone in even the most mundane conversation. Try as I might to disassociate myself from the mean-spirited voices in the next room, these men exuded disgust at my presence and a palpable desire for me to leave them the hell alone.

The three of us lay side by side in silence. I tried to induce sleep in myself by imitation and had almost forgotten that Cass lay beside me when, with a shock, I felt her touch my hand. She reached for it tentatively and then stroked it outright with a single bold finger. Then, in infinitesimal movements, she brought her face close to my ear. I could smell her perfume enveloping me and feel her breath on my hair.

"Sorry," she whispered, stroking and stroking my hand with a single finger. "Sorry, sorry, sorry, sorry, sorry." She breathed it over and over, and even in the pathetic whisper there was mockery. I nearly strangled trying to keep my breathing steady, imitating sleep.

In the morning, when I woke, she was lying practically on top of Michael. Inches of room separated her from me in my cramped place against the wall. The proprietor woke me an hour before the train was due. He shook them too, but they refused to be roused, as belligerent in sleep as awake. I slid away from them and at the door glanced back into the sad little bedroom to see them sprawled like two suicides accidentally discovered. I had two cups of coffee and reached the station just as the train was becoming visible down the track.

In Teheran I was lucky enough to hear them check into the honeycomb-like whorehouse hotel where the hippie travelers stayed, and any time I started to leave my room, I peered into the hallway through a crack in the door to make sure I wouldn't run into them. I succeeded in avoiding them, but as memory would have it, Cassandra had pressed herself into my brain and never left me.

It's not until years have passed that you can tell which moments you have lived through will remain permanently embedded, and another lengthy time must pass before you even begin to understand why. For me that day and night in Ezurum formed a permanent track that spelled "warning," and recounting it here I chose to disguise the ruined woman I met there with the name Cassandra to underscore the role she played in my life.

On reflection, it seemed obvious that she was a smart, book-loving woman of language. There must have been more conversation of the normal sort that has faded beyond recollection, because somehow I know she was a well-known journalist back home in Manhattan who wrote on popular culture. I even think I had read some of her stuff and considered it witty, even hilarious in parts. She had used her way with words to become a professional wiseacre, but her desperate meanness seemed to suggest that she had failed to invent a foundation to her life that kept her anchored to the earth. I sensed then and still believe that Cassandra's killing cynicism and corroding bitterness were tied to the total waste of her gift of language.

When I watched Cassandra empty her bag that day, I recognized in her a fellow book lover. We were members of the same club, readers who escaped whole portions of life by diving into novels. We used linear fantasies like alternative realities, pulling them over our heads when life became too intense. We entered books like nonreaders entered sleep—and often entered them *instead* of entering sleep.

But until the late sixties, nearly all the alternative realities into which we voracious female readers dove were realities created by men. After two decades of outpourings in which the voices of female writers have gained volume and their stories have gained shape, it's hard to remember a time when nearly all the books told men's stories. Intelligent, educated, even gifted, at the end of the sixties we were all Cassandras wildly pulling books out of our bags. We were searching in vain for our reflections in the waters of a hurtling river, but just ahead out of sight was a place— an eddy with its own distinctive rhythms and directions— where, finally, we could begin to plumb our own depths.

SEVEN

Apprenticeship

I returned to the San Francisco Bay Area with my restlessness redoubled. I could only decide what I *didn't* want to do—I was certainly no scholar, and had no call as a teacher. I sublet a railroad flat in San Francisco's Haight-Ashbury district, and set about to find a job.

In 1969 leaving my flat to look for a job was like sneaking out of one world to another—or a small galaxy of others—in a commuter's spaceship. I say "sneaking" because of the costumes: everybody was disguised in costumes then, even if unintentionally. Dressing for job interviews was a challenging exercise in imagination, since the jobs I went in for spanned a handful of the clashing, crashing themes of the day. Over the course of the summer, I tried to be a nighttime drug counselor for teenage runaways; secretary at World Without War, which counseled conscientious objectors and offered safe haven to draft dodgers; marketing assistant in an HMO, a concept so new that a major portion of the job was explaining it; "Girl Friday" (thank God *that* term has been retired) to a rock impresario; and technical editor at Bechtel, an international engineering firm whose communications department was staffed by a band of guerrilla poets subsidizing their writing lives by working for the enemy and looting its writing supplies. At the ring of the phone, I went from handmade sandals to spool heels, pantyhose (newly invented) and short skirts, to Katharine Hepburn slacks and a blazer.

Who the hell was I, anyway? I'd spent six years in college and traveled the world, but what was my work going to be? Picking my way through the amazing scene on Haight Street, which was already past its high-spirited prime, these fundamental questions seemed more like social issues than my own personal quest. There were flower children with a used-up air propped against storefronts; wild-eyed, wild-haired hippies talking out loud to themselves; Diggers in headbands passing out food; mumbling spare-change junkies hanging, sick, against mailboxes; beautiful young women in gauzy dresses, their breasts and often their hugely pregnant bellies on view in the morning sun; young black men in black clothes and opaque sunglasses, their expressions made mysteriously blank by the hiding of their eyes. Who *were* we all, flung out there on the grungy sidewalk in the pounding August sunshine of Haight Street? Half a world away, the war in Vietnam dragged on, siphoning off boys and then casting the survivors back to drift on city streets like this one. Long-haired veterans and draft evaders in combat clothes threaded through the scene, the emotion of their stories buried behind flat eyes.

As I waited for my bus in this milling stew of identities, I read the photocopied messages that hung in tatters on the telephone poles: "Anyone knowing the whereabouts of Ann J_____ . . . " "Marty B_____ , please come home. We love you, Dad, Mom, and Peg." "Janet L _____ , last seen Boulder, Colorado, Christmas Day 1967, your mother is ill. Your father is worried. Please call home."

These messages rang with sad uncertainty—what tone do you strike when you call out into the midst of two hundred million people in the hope of reaching a runaway child? Everyone on the street seemed under thirty and cut off at the roots. "Remember," went the cliché of the day, "today is the first day of the rest of your life." That was enough to strike terror in anybody's heart.

Nothing on the merry-go-round of the sixties had eradicated in me the sense that I could do some kind of work with the written word. I pulled myself together and pounded on the door of the publishing industry, and there I lucked out in an unforeseen way.

To a raft of heartfelt letters asking how, in publishing, a book lover with no interest in teaching might be useful, I received a single telephone response. "Miss Lipsett," the caller shouted with no preliminary remarks, "have you any interest at all in working like a canine for very little money? In doing things the old-fashioned way, learning to turn, by the sweat of your brow, a manuscript into a book? I am simply worn out, disgusted, by the thought of interviewing one more East Coast transplant who considers it below his or her station to read proof or check corrections. If you follow through on your query, you will learn that reading proof and checking corrections very nearly form the heart and soul of publishing. You can't *do* the job if you don't know the book. From your letter I considered it possible that you might be interested in what amounts to a book publishing apprenticeship."

Had anyone *ever* spoken so precisely, so *grammatically,* carefully attending to and blending (I was to learn these components) intention, meaning, rhythm, efficiency, and grace of language? Moreover, the caller boomed. I pictured Joseph Stalin and only just managed to make an appointment. It was a wonderful coincidence: I was seeking my life's work, and Willis L. Parker was looking for a serf.

If he boomed on the phone, he loomed in person. He was a large, well-built man in his early sixties with a shiny, hairless dome, rather natty suspenders, and affectations.

He had been editing book manuscripts for forty years. By the time he died, he had been editing for sixty-five years, and he never got tired, or never admitted to getting tired, of stacking and squaring off a new manuscript in front of himself on the desk, lining up the accoutrements of his trade, and putting that first decisive mark between the lines on page one.

That mark, in accordance with his highly personalized editing style, was distinctive. He did indeed come from the old school: he believed in inkwells. So all of the editors he trained over his long career in book publishing may have had a wide array of photographs and cultural icons on the bulletin boards *above* their desks, but upon them were the same items lined up in a row—an old-fashioned pen in an inkwell (filled on request by WLP himself, with red ink from a gallon jug and a funnel); a tiny brown medicine bottle with a rubber stopper that looked as if it had come from a Dickens-era chemist's shop; a stack of gummed editor's flags that had to be licked (Post-its, second only to pantyhose in their liberating usefulness for the working woman, were far in the future); and a bouquet of Q-tips in a little cup.

The point was to edit in ink, to convey in a way mere pencil never could an authoritative, decisive tone. At the same time, one had to provide for occasional lapses—even editors with half a century behind them made mistakes (so he boomed, anyway, though whenever one of us fledglings spotted an error or oversight of his, we had palpitations of guilt).

So, in the little brown bottle was bleach, also refillable from a jug in WLP's sanctum. If one made a mistake, one dipped a Q-tip in the bleach and touched it carefully to the red-inked mark on the page. Instantly, *instantly,* the red disappeared—and the level of precision you could achieve was amazing. You could touch away a period, or the tail on a Q, or change a semicolon to a comma with a single dab. Or you could wipe out a whole page's worth of red interlinear changes without a trace, though you'd have to wait for the page to dry, or the tip of your pen would dig furry holes in the paper when you tried again. Watching the bleach drink up the red ink on the page was every bit as fascinating then as it is now to watch the cursor run backwards across a computer screen, mowing down words.

Nineteen sixty-nine was still years before editors came to use computers, but when they did, a long time after I had met Bill—we never really *called* him WLP, but he signed like that—he told me a story from his earliest publishing job that threw more than the industry into perspective: it conveyed something endearing about the world. It seemed in our own time that publishers would soon be requiring writers to submit their manuscripts on disks, so writers who were resisting the new technology or who were unable to afford a computer were fearful of losing their ability to ply their trade. But as Bill remembered, when he was twenty-two or so, touch typing had appeared on the scene. And some publishers, Bill's university press among them, were requiring that manuscripts—note: *man*uscripts—be submitted in typescript form.

"And you never heard such a commotion," Bill huffed in his Victorian way. "The professors came to the steps of the press and threw up a picket line. They accused the press of elitism, of favoring those wealthy gentlemen writers who could afford to hire young ladies to type their work. They never *dreamed* of learning to type themselves, you understand. Well, that polite picket line shook the venerable board members and caused them to lose considerable sleep. I believe, if I can trust my memory, that the board indeed backed down."

When he told me this, I was copy editing for a computer magazine, and asked him to write it up. Why he compromised his considerable dignity by admitting to me that he wrote eight drafts before giving up, I don't know. But I understood by then that he was such a born editor, so critical and intolerant of ambiguity, he could never have written the smallest piece—and he admitted once that, sad as he was to be separated from his grown children and much as he hated to talk on the phone after using it all day at work, he loathed writing letters and wouldn't. Though he passionately loved language, he couldn't play in it, ever. What he could do was follow others along, grooming their ideas with exquisite skill and care.

That and teach young editors to use the tools of the trade.

My first day on the job he set me the task of copy editing a four-hundred-page anthropology manuscript that the company had published years before. He pulled it down from a high, high shelf, where it had lain for years in a box marked "Dead." He handed me that and intoned, "One."

Then he led me to the podium in the hall that held *Webster's International Dictionary, Second Edition,* and enunciated, "Two."

Then he brought me the vaunted inkwell, the flags, the little brown bottle, and the cluster of Q-tips, and said, "Three."

A final set of essentials was delivered with the solemnity of an ecclesiastical ritual: a dual set of books—*The Chicago Manual of Style,* and an ancient tome, copyright 1948, called *Words into Type.* "Four. It's all you'll need—ever. When you're finished, come back down the hall and show me what you could do."

I ventured to mention that I knew very little about anthropology.

"Perfect. You're a model reader. Whatever you stumble over, edit. Whatever you don't understand, query. Precision, rhythm, efficiency, clarity, and grace. Confirm the spelling of every proper noun. Query the spelling of every specialized term. *Excise jargon.* And *never* make a change you cannot justify, chapter and verse," he growled, with a tap on the two books in my hands and a nod to the dictionary in the hall.

It took more than a month, and the interrogation he gave me nearly left *me* with the word *dead* stamped across my forehead. Two more weeks to correct my work after he had reviewed it, and he grudgingly suggested that I might have a few of the makings of a competent manuscript editor. Might.

Then he handed me my next task, a floppy set of page proofs of a textbook on modern Russian history and a tiny hard-back book called *Indexing,* which looked a hundred years old. "Read this," he said. "Then do everything it tells you to do."

As I left his office, I followed his inadvertent glance at one of his bookshelves and saw there the published book that corresponded to the page proofs I now held in my hands. Its size made me shudder, and it undoubtedly already had a mammoth index whose Rs alone ran ten printed pages.

It took me six more weeks to learn how to build an index in my mind as I read and marked up the proof. As the little blue book instructed, I recorded every entry and subentry on a separate three-by-five card cut in half. When I was halfway through the ells, he came in and put me out of my misery. "Type it up and we'll take a look at it," he told me. Another week spent cleaning and tightening the index, and I was in full possession of a book art I'd never even thought about before I'd met Bill Parker. What's more, I learned to understand a thing line by line, thought by thought, that I never had a name for until I saw a computer rendering of a building some years later. It was the architecture of a book, the ideas isolated and strung together by logic, the whole thing as delicate and magnificently complex as a spider's web deep inside my mind. It required more grit and endurance than I ever thought I had to hold the thing together for the time it took to get it down on the cards.

"A beauty," he boomed, glowering at the lists of entries on my final draft, and my knees actually weakened in relief.

Boot camp for editors. Skill by skill, book part by book part, publishing phase by publishing phase, he took me through the process, and eventually I began to work on *live* manuscripts sent in to me by living authors. I went through many brown bottles of bleach struggling to help rather than hurt, and having him review the editing on my first real project was slow hell. I never gained the knack of shooting down authors outright—and I'm not sure WLP, for all his stuffy gruffness, ever killed authors or ideas either. Rather, he fostered in all his apprentice editors an abiding respect for writers and considered the editor to be in the writer's service—perhaps his most old-fashioned but increasingly radical idea.

I learned nuts-and-bolts, on-the-page editing and the time-honored process that transforms a manuscript into a book. I did come to coax some books into print. And I left after several years with a toolkit full of skills. Without my even knowing it, WLP had enabled me to become what I would be for the next twenty-four years and am still: a midwife of books.

But there was something more: the next step in my lifelong, interminably slow internal evolution as a writer. Bill Parker articulated for me and fostered my deep appreciation for the qualities that distinguished carefully crafted prose: precision, clarity, efficiency, rhythm, and—I always thought he gave this one a spin, because it was his wife's name—grace.

EIGHT

Reading Women

I was standing in the check-out line in the Ashby Avenue Co-op in Berkeley with a bag full of produce stamped *organic,* when I suddenly recognized the woman ahead of me in line as a high-school classmate.

"Carol?" I ventured, marveling. She had always been beautiful, and she turned a face to me as elegant and reserved as the moon, yet vulnerable too. I was dazzled.

"How *are* you?" she asked me. "What are you doing now?"

I had recently moved to Berkeley. I told her about my job in publishing.

"If you're involved with books, maybe you'd be interested in a class I'm trying to put together," she said. "On women's fiction. I'm trying to start a group."

"Women's fiction."

"Yes. Women writers. Only."

"Mmmm." It was 1969. Reticence and resistance, even suspicion, rose up in me like a brick wall.

The first book I'd read was *Toby Tyler*, about a little boy who joins the circus. The book that lay open on my loft bed was *Magister Ludi*, by Hermann Hesse. Stacked at the foot were *East of Eden*, by John Steinbeck; *The Colossus of Maroussi*, by Henry Miller; *On the Road*, by Jack Kerouac; *The Rainbow*, by D. H. Lawrence; *The Adventures of Augie March*, by Saul Bellow; *Catch-22*, by Joseph Heller; and a skinny volume of *Howl*, by Allen Ginsberg.

In my last graduate seminar before I'd bolted and flown to Africa, the professor had spent three hours each evening sorting the imagery in novels into two categories. Trees, rain, canoes, *writers* he deemed penetrating male images. Earth, fields, pools, *readers*—these were passive, receptive, and female. Another professor raised a great laugh by characterizing *Jane Eyre* as a novel written by one sex-starved ball-breaker about another. It was generally agreed, in the book circles I had been running in, that the great tragedy of *Jane Eyre* was not Jane's isolated singularity and the waste of her intelligence, but the emasculation of Mr. Rochester; that Jane Austen wrote solely to ease her neurotic anxiety and hid her work from her family with shame; and that Emily Dickinson was out-and-out crazy, a classic case of a reader born, to her fatal misfortune, with a writer's gifts.

But this was Berkeley 1969. Since I had first come to Berkeley from the silent suburbs, the city had been alive with voices speaking and singing and shouting out—the free speech movement, the civil rights movement, the antiwar movement, the black power movement, the independent living movement, the birth of the Peace and Freedom party, and the wild surge of drugs and rock music known as the

Gathering of the Tribes, which marked the invention of the counterculture. What were the sixties but a time of giving voice to the unspoken, unheard, and unsung? And now a new set of voices was rising up from small groups of women who had been geared for change by the issues of the times only to find themselves butting up against restrictive roles and closed doors still marked "Men."

The variegated community of Berkeley swirled around Carol and me as we stood talking in front of the registers. It was the whole chorus come to market—from stringy adult skateboarders to elderly long-time householders; from goofed-out hippies to glowering bikers in jean jackets with the arms torn off; from proud blacks in dashikis to frighteningly gray-skinned mystics in tall white turbans; from mumbling winos to professors in tweeds, picking up wine to take to dinner parties; from children living in school busses with their own children, named Summer, Spring, and Sparrow, to intellectuals who composed their books in silent, stately houses behind stone pillars; from long-haired girls in granny dresses suckling their toddlers to the wives of young professionals pushing their bonneted babies in airstream strollers; from psychotic mumblers to hallucinating acid-heads to bewildered runaways floating without direction through the city in a stoned-out haze. Everyone came to the Co-op for food, gossip, and information. The cold linoleum could have been the hard-packed dust of an East African farmers' market. The fluorescent lights could have been the sunshine beating through baobab trees. Though twenty-two years have passed, I can still see Carol standing in this profusion as clear as day. She was wearing a

long black-and-white Moroccan hooded cape and tall
leather boots, and inviting me to listen to a whole chorus
of voices that—unbelievable, given what they came to
mean!—had not yet come clear to me.

We began with Sappho.

> Don't ask me what to wear
> I have no embroidered
> headband from Sardis to
> give you, Cleis, such as
> I wore
>
> and my mother
> always said that in her
> day a purple ribbon
> looped in the hair was thought
> to be high style indeed
>
> but we were dark:
> a girl
> whose hair is yellower than
> torchlight should wear no
> headdress but fresh flowers[1]

Ten or twelve women sat in a circle in my little front
room.

"Sappho was a great poet," said Carol. She took her role
as teacher and guide into this unexplored territory with seriousness. "Only a few fragments of her poems have sur-
vived, and yet they convey both her mastery and her

'otherness'—her womanly concerns and the distinctly female qualities of her voice."

"But, um, wasn't she a lesbian?" someone asked nervously. That gay liberation would become a potent social movement was then unimaginable. Not only were the voices arising from the first consciousness-raising groups accused of stridency and whininess, but—so the innuendoes had it—they were skirting dangerously close to butch.

"Do you have something against lesbians?" demanded a heavy-set woman. Defiantly she threw her arm around the neck of a wiry, long-haired woman in shorts and heavy boots. "That poem is my life story. Don't ask *me* what to wear. I've been wearing overalls ever since I ripped off my Mary Janes and threw them into the river. I don't think I've worn a skirt since I left home."

Agitation rippled through the group.

"But you're missing the point," said Carol. "Think about it. These poems are twenty-five hundred years old. Twenty-five centuries. And Sappho's voice is so familiar, she could be sitting in this room. What her words convey isn't a lesbian sensibility, it's a *female* sensibility. Female passions and interests. Passions, interests, tones of voice, aspects of the emotional life that have remained consistent across the centuries. Don't you see? It's been there all along."

She read another poem, and we sat listening to Sappho whistling down through the ages, trailing a purple ribbon, to slip into our circle.

> He is more than a hero
> He is a god in my eyes—

the man who is allowed
to sit beside you—he

who listens intimately
to the sweet murmur of
your voice, the enticing

laughter that makes my own
heart beat fast. If I meet
you suddenly, I can't

speak—my tongue is broken;
a thin flame runs under
my skin; seeing nothing,

hearing only my own ears
drumming, I drip with sweat;
trembling shakes my body

and I turn paler than
dry grass. At such times
death isn't far from me[2]

I, for one, was struck dumb. I was no prude; still, even
at the age of twenty-six my notion of lesbians was restricted
to stereotypes of gym teachers and maiden aunts. But the
San Francisco Bay Area was becoming a haven for gays (before the word became generally used) who wished to live
openly, without deception. Somehow or other I became
aware that not one but two lesbian couples numbered in
the first group that all but filled my living room. And we
were all struck silent—the heterosexual women in the
room every bit as threatened as most straight men in the

nineties by the possibility that we would all be mistaken for gay. I wondered whether it was all that wise to go on with this business of women writers.

"Seems like an interesting place to start," said Carol, into the awkward silence. "I planned a roughly historical reading list, but let's wait for that. For our next meeting read *The Well of Loneliness,* by Radclyffe Hall. Be prepared for some purple prose and a mannered way of writing. Trust me. It will be worthwhile."

It was the saddest book, a deeply romantic tale of unrequited love between a young woman named Stephen Gordon, who had been raised by her loving father as a son, and the woman who became the object of her passionate desire. True to its title, the book was less about love than about the profound loneliness of a young woman unable to live by the suffocating rules of femininity. The unqualified familiarity of that predicament melted our defensiveness and congealed the group. I read the book avidly, but with a feeling that life as I knew it would no longer be possible.

I thought about the obvious and was amazed: I had read the usual "girl" books. The standouts for me had been *The Five Little Pepper* books, *The Secret Garden, Little Women,* and *Jo's Boys,* and all the Sue Barton and Cherry Ames nursing books I could find. At eleven I gained access to the Junior Adult section of the library. Though I wish I could say I gagged on the primers there on how to be a fifties-style teenage girl, I gorged on them until I stumbled on a raunchy potboiler shelved by mistake, owing to its title, with the Junior Adult books. Called *Senior Spring,* it was a steamy, detailed account of the sexual curricula of a fraternity house as it plowed its way systematically through the campus population of sweater-set coeds. Throughout my teenage years, I had plucked books off the shelf and dived into them nightly. Scene after scene inscribed itself on my memory, but none so indelibly (nor so often) as the athletically sexy, outrageously explicit party scenes from *Senior Spring*—and how that book ever made it into print, let alone onto the prim Junior Adult shelf during the buttoned-up fifties, I'll never know. When I first got my hands on it, in 1957, I was fourteen.

Day and night, for as long as I could stay awake and all the way through college and graduate school, I had been stretching out flat every day and immersing myself in novels. And by that year, 1969, when I was twenty-six years old, perhaps five of the total—all right, maybe *ten*—had been serious books by women. Reading *The Well of Loneliness* was like taking an elevator down to the basement of a building you think you know. There were boilers and machines and all sorts of things going on down there that had nothing to do with sexual preference. Everybody seemed to feel it, and we were launched.

We took our cue from the consciousness-raising groups mushrooming around us and resisted the wifely urge to bring food. "Let's keep focused on the books, and what we're doing here," Carol exhorted us in her mild but self-assured way. "Food is for parties."

Instead we had a Babette's Feast of books.

Fast forward twenty-three years. It is Berkeley 1992, shortly after Anita Hill testified before the Senate Judiciary Committee and quietly threw out the first ball in a whole new game. Over the course of the decades, four of us from the original reading group have reconnected, and this Sunday morning in May, we have called a reunion to reminisce. We meet at the Bateau Ivre, a homey restaurant with a garden and brick walls. Open since the early seventies, it looks disconcertingly unchanged.

Carol, our teacher, is still a lunar beauty, pale and calm. She has remained unerringly literary—went on to create with others the first two major anthologies of women's poetry and to translate Sartre's five volumes of criticism on Flaubert, among other books. Kay too—once a serious, childlike girl with straight, swinging hair and an air of deep seriousness—looks miraculously unmarked, but is more full of jokes and cheer now. She's an attorney for the state of California. Gail, a poet turned technical editor, is my longtime friend. I have asked them to meet me here and brainstorm—I want to reconstruct our reading list and find out what it turned out to have meant.

"Meant?" says Kay, with her dark brows raised. "Reading women in the group meant everything to me. It completely changed my life. I was still reeling from my college adviser's refusal to recommend me for medical school. He told me to go to nursing school instead so I wouldn't get married and waste a place that could have gone to a *real* medical student. I just don't think I ever got over that. But the books! Reading those books was like the lifting of a gray fog. Suddenly I saw that other people, in the books and in the group, felt and thought things I had felt and thought. Maybe it was just that we were growing up, but I don't think so. After all, we were in our late twenties by then. But when I think of myself before we read those women, I think of a person completely lost, wandering around in a deep gray fog, very much alone."

Her words bring back a memory of Cassandra lying in that usurped bed between her dead drunk boyfriend and me. In my memory she seemed too far gone to be redeemed by any word or book. I was sure I'd been saved from her fate by the sudden serendipitous meeting with Carol and the revelation of all those women's stories.

"One thing I remember," says Gail, "was how we clung to those books. We said we weren't a *woman's group,* we weren't a *consciousness-raising group,* we were a *reading* group. Oh, yes, we talked about all the unsayables—until then, unsayables. Once we talked about jealousy, I remember. About jealousy between women and what *that* was all about. And about friendship, and passion, and dying for love. About the pain of love and the terrible losses within marriage. About equality and egalitarian relationships— about *respect,* and how it got translated between men and women. About fathers. About husbands and boyfriends and friends. And about *work*—at least, we *began* to talk about work then. And of course about sex—didn't we even read Masters and Johnson?"

"Oh, yes," I crow, "we *binged* on Masters and Johnson. And even more so on *Our Bodies, Ourselves*—which told us more in a month about our bodies and our feelings about our bodies than had been common knowledge *ever*. The politics of orgasm! That book was the end of the Dark Ages, and thank God we were young enough to enjoy it!"

"Oh, *yes*," cries Gail, "that's just what I mean. We talked and talked and *talked* about things, and we all said we were talking about the books. I'd say we talked about the books for a year before we actually admitted we were talking about ourselves and the deepest concerns of our lives. In fact, I can remember when it happened . . . "

She stops and gazes off. All four of us look past each other, turning over memories of meeting after meeting of passionate book talk, trying to guess what she would pull out of the deep past.

"It might have been when we were reading Sylvia Plath . . . "

"Yes, I think I remember what you mean," I say. We had read *Ariel* and *The Bell Jar,* finding raw pain and cutting irony struggling on every page.

"We were all standing up to go and suddenly we were talking, *really* talking, about loneliness . . . "

Ping! I remember it. It was not fashionable to be lonely in the sixties. This was the time, after all, when we all came together on the streets to protest the war, and in Golden Gate Park to affirm our membership in one or another of the tribes that made up the counterculture. And yet . . .

It is as if a plug has been pulled from my memory. "Do you remember the woman in the group whose husband wouldn't let her come to the meetings anymore?" I ask. The other three squint—they can't quite remember, but I can *see* this woman. We met in her house. She had small children, and the air around her shook with the kind of agitation I recognize now as frazzled motherhood at dinnertime. Her clothes were rumpled, her black hair was ratted out huge and thin, like a big cloud around her head that you could see through. We had all filed in and sat around the living room, when she came flying out of the kitchen shaking with rage. "The son-of-a-bitch is making me quit the group. I can't do this anymore."

A man came out behind her. "Listen, no—" he protested.

"No, goddamit," she shrieked at him. "Tell them the truth. You said no to me so you can say no to them. You've got to leave," she said to us, and waved her hands. I guess we just filed out and left. All I can remember is the barely contained hatred for each other in the eyes of those two as the children careened around them and they stood there, poised for battle, waiting for us to leave.

We talk and talk and succeed in reconstructing the list. Though we are sure there are gaps, and every few minutes somebody thinks of one more, we agree it went something like this:

> Charlotte Brontë, *Jane Eyre*
> Emily Brontë, *Wuthering Heights*
> George Sand, *Carlotta*
> George Eliot, *Middlemarch*
> Emily Dickinson, *Poems*
> Virginia Woolf, *Mrs. Dalloway, To the Lighthouse,*

Orlando, The Waves, and *A Room of One's Own*

Kate Chopin, *The Awakening*

Charlotte Perkins Gilman, *The Yellow Wallpaper*

Edith Wharton, *House of Mirth*

Willa Cather, *My Antonia* and *Song of the Lark*

Djuna Barnes, *Nightwood*

Anaïs Nin, volume four of the *Diaries* and *Delta of Venus*

Marguerite Duras, *Hiroshima Mon Amour*

Simone de Beauvoir, *Prime of Life* and *Second Sex*

Flannery O'Conner, *Everything That Rises Must Converge*

Carson McCullers, *Member of the Wedding*

Harper Lee, *To Kill a Mockingbird*

Doris Lessing, *The Golden Notebook* and *The Four-Gated City*

Anne Sexton, *All My Pretty Ones*

Sylvia Plath, *Ariel* and *The Bell Jar*

J, *The Story of O*

Jean Rhys, *The Wide Sargasso Sea* and *Quartet*

Masters and Johnson, *Human Sexual Response*

The Boston Women's Health Collective, *Our Bodies, Ourselves*

Edna O'Brien, *The Country Girls*

Joan Didion, *Play It as It Lays*

Rita Mae Brown, *Rubyfruit Jungle*

May Sarton, *Journal of a Solitude*

Isak Dineson, *Out of Africa*

Olive Schreiner, *Stories from an African Farm*

There could have been more, many more. It's been twenty-three years, after all. We sit over our empty brunch plates, settled into the past and grazing there. "I remember . . . " says one, then another one, and each draws forth a particular moment. All the memories are similar, ideas floating toward us from a long time ago. "There was another time when we were leaving," says Gail, "and we all stood at the door for an hour or so. I think we had to talk about a book for a few hours as a way of moving in on something personal. Then we talked about rape, do you remember?" asks Gail. And I can see the doorframe as clear as anything—and remember that for many years before that night I couldn't say the word *rape* out loud.

One circle comes back to me, when suddenly the war sprang alive, blood spurting and gushing, pain searing, children screaming. It was over the news of My Lai—our own soldiers' frenzied massacre of a South Vietnamese village. They burned the huts and left dead and dying villagers in a pile. *Life* magazine published pictures of the slaughter. For four years I had stood with other protesters on university campuses and outside draft boards as the Antiwar movement grew, and time after time I had joined the rivers of marchers flowing down the major thoroughfares of Berkeley and San Francisco. But I had been marching out of anger and concern for my draft-age friends and only an abstract notion of the war's reality. Never until that moment, primed by Simone de Beauvoir's account of occupied Paris during World War II, did the tangle of pain, terror, burnt skin, shattered bones, lost children, and tragically disrupted normalcy that was war leave my head and enter my heart. We talked for a long time that night, not leaving but sitting together, grateful for and unwilling to leave the circle.

The books opened us all to many realities far deeper and more mysterious than the received version of late-sixties life in Berkeley. I began, after our meetings, to sit in my green stuffed chair with pen and paper in hand, fighting a kind of primitive embarrassment I have learned to recognize well. It is the embarrassment of the novice about to admit desire. There was no one there to see me, but having roared through *A Room of One's Own* twice, I was about to admit to myself and to the yellow legal pad clipped squarely onto the writing board on my lap that, in my own mind, if I failed to become a writer, my life would have been a waste. With Virginia Woolf a cottage industry now, it's hard to remember the passion that her small book on women's writing could evoke, but the mental breathlessness with which I read it was as rare as it was precious, and I knew it.

At our table at the Bateau Ivre, we four divvy up the check and stand to leave. We ask a man at a table behind us to take our picture against the brick fireplace. ("Why shouldn't we ask him?" whispers Gail. "He's been lapping up every word we've said for the past two and a half hours.") "By the way," says Kay, on our way out. "Did anyone see the play of *A Room of One's Own*?"

"Oh!" I say, in rapture. I had seen it on PBS. The actress captured perfectly the magical marriage of grace and

directness as she looked straight into the camera and spoke the master's words:

> I told you in the course of this paper that Shakespeare had a sister; but do not look for her in Sir Sidney Lee's life of the poet. She died young—alas she never wrote a word. She lies buried where the omnibuses now stop, opposite the Elephant and Castle. Now my belief is that this poet who never wrote a word and was buried at the crossroads still lives. She lives in you and in me, and in many other women who are not here tonight, for they are washing up the dishes and putting the children to bed. But she lives; for great poets do not die; they are continuing presences; they need only the opportunity to walk among us in the flesh. This opportunity, as I think, it is now coming within your power to give her. For my belief is that if we live another century or so—I am talking of the common life which is the real life and not of the little separate lives which we live as individuals—and have five hundred a year each of us and rooms of our own; if we have the habit of freedom and the courage to write exactly what we think; if we escape a little from the common sitting-room and see human beings not always in their relation to each other but in relation to reality; and the sky, too, and the trees or whatever it may be in themselves; if we look past Milton's bogey, for no human being should shut out the view; if we face the fact, for it is a fact, that there is no arm to cling to, but that we go alone and that our relation is to the world of reality and not only to the world of men and women, then the opportunity will come and the dead poet who was Shakespeare's sister will put on the body which she has so often laid down. Drawing her life from the lives of the unknown who were her forerunners, as her brother did before her, she will

be born. As for her coming without that preparation, without that effort on our part, without that determination that when she is born again she shall find it possible to live and write her poetry, that we cannot expect, for that would be impossible. But I maintain that she would come if we worked for her, and that so to work, even in poverty and obscurity, is worthwhile.[3]

"My God, I'm *doing* it," I said to my TV screen, three published novels and twenty-three years after I first read that passage.

"I cried," I tell the others.

"Who didn't?" asked Kay.

"Thank God for Shakespeare's sister," one of us breathes. And so we book women of the godless sixties end our delightful reunion with a prayer.

1. From Mary Barnard, *Sappho: A New Translation* (Berkeley: Univ. of California Press, 1958), #39.

2. Barnard, *Sappho,* #83.

3. Virginia Woolf, *A Room of One's Own* (New York: Harcourt Brace Jovanovich, 1929; Harvest/HBJ paperback), 117–18.

NINE

Writing Mothers

I must have been one of the few aspiring female writers who didn't read Tillie Olsen's *Silences* when it came out in 1978. Not that I hadn't heard of it—among women writers and readers the book inspired the kind of excited book gossip I thrived on and brought relief to many who ardently hoped and dreamed of writing some day. But I was afraid of the book—with courage and anger, it looked directly at the social forces that suppressed poor voices, workers' voices, and above all female voices. With my belated desire to write rising slowly over the decade—finding intermittent expression in a poem here, an image there, an increasing series of book reviews that actually saw print—I quaked at the idea of focusing on anything that might discourage or seduce me from the path.

Had I acquainted myself with *Silences,* or any of the feminist criticism that had begun to emerge at the time, I would have read what it took me many years to realize:

Indeed, in our century as in the last, until very recently almost all distinguished achievement has come from childless women: Willa Cather, Ellen Glasgow, Gertrude Stein, Edith Wharton, Virginia Woolf, Elizabeth Bowen, Katherine Mansfield, Isak Dinesen, Katherine Anne Porter, Dorothy Richardson, Henry Handel Richardson, Susan Glaspell, Dorothy Parker, Lillian Hellman, Eudora Welty, Djuna Barnes, Anaïs Nin, Ivy Compton-Burnett, Zora Neale Hurston, Elizabeth Madox Roberts, Christina Stead, Carson McCullers, Flannery O'Connor, Jean Stafford, May Sarton, Josephine Herbst, Jessamyn West, Janet Frame, Lillian Smith, Iris Murdoch, Joyce Carol Oates, Hannah Green, Lorraine Hansberry.[1]

All, all, were daughters, none mothers.

I looked up as I crossed the street at Telegraph and Russell, and there—in another of her surprise appearances—was Carol. It was 1973. I had seen her in London on a long trip I'd taken to break the grip of the commuter's life, but the reading group had long ago dispersed. With Tom, the man in my life, I was soon to head out of Berkeley to make a new start in a town in Marin County, north of the Golden Gate Bridge. And yet here, like a warning, was Carol: same Moroccan cape with its tasseled hood, same high leather boots, same elegant face—like a symbol, a reminder, of the womanly life of the mind.

And roundly, extravagantly pregnant—*Carol!* What had happened to the celebration of ideas, of the voices emerging from obscurity? I think I looked at her straining belly with something like disappointment, if not outright disgust. I flagged her down, we stood and chatted, I even put my hands on her belly to feel a kick. Supposedly grown up, I still felt like a child betrayed by a friend who has gone over to stand with the big girls. Well, that's that, I thought. The world turns.

Only slightly less retro than getting pregnant in the first half of the seventies was the experience of being swept away by love. Yet unexpectedly a solid friendship had grown, widened, deepened, and—the way a slowly sinking ship suddenly disappears—I was swallowed up. I was thirty— ludicrously late by all the old scripts. But, to use Carolyn Heilbrun's heart-lifting phrases, in those days we were all quite consciously reinventing womanhood and writing our individual lives. A spinster? Hardly. When Tom and I moved across the Bay to start a new life together, I considered myself something of a feminist pioneer.

Three years later, living with Tom and patching together a livelihood from freelance editing and occasional book reviewing, I saw in the eyes of some of my single friends that my own pregnancy was inspiring emotional dust devils similar to those I had experienced on seeing Carol. What on earth was I *do*ing? I was no sort of mother—held housework in the highest contempt, read rather than cleaned, wrote rather than cooked. Similarly, Tom. A photographer by passion, a printer by trade, he was as independent and barely domesticated as a bobcat and often went off with his oversized camera for wilderness trips on his own. He had the voice of a cowboy, the mild eyes of a patient man, and an understated humor as dry and light as a tumbleweed.

In those first years of our life together, Tom was no more homebound than I. Despite our straitened circumstances, we both tended toward restaurant fare and extravagant presents. The joy of my life was finding myself living with a man pursuing his work in the darkroom as passionately and for as many hours as I pursued my own in the bedroom, hunched over the typewriter or poring over a book.

I could struggle over a story or book review, then edit and read in bed for hours before I fell asleep, all with the delicious anticipation of waking up some time in the middle of the night next to Tom. He would be sleeping the sleep of a man driven by his own demons to ignore his exhaustion and stand in the red glow of the dark light until the morning hours. As the baby grew to quite an alarming size within me, he no doubt shared my trepidations as to what would happen next.

With the arrival of the baby, for a time, all else dropped away.

I suppose that sudden transition from a child's to a parent's reality has been well-documented, and that before Sam's birth I simply glided over such accounts with unseeing eyes. One book I read, among the many forgettable ones, stands out in my memory as having conveyed some of what I experienced—*Mother Knot,* by Jane Lazarre, a hilariously straight-spoken account of a journalist who finally manages to take a year off to write a novel only to become pregnant and then give birth to an energetic little boy.

But something deeper, more fundamental, and completely unexpected happened to us when we had our baby. Although I write here only for myself, Tom too carried a deep scar across his childhood like the one scored across mine by my mother's death. I believe that the very feel of our baby's skin, the sound of his cry in the night, the depth of his gaze as he stared mildly up at us with infancy's utter lack of self-awareness—these flesh-and-blood experiences worked on us, seeping in under and around our creative concerns like healing vapors. To our great surprise, we took to parenthood like cats—gazing, licking, grooming, rolling, and playing in a family heap. Within my soul, ripped places began to knit together, and the feminist in me was shaken to feel moments of unexpected, unimagined joy. For the first time ever, I felt sure I knew my mother—she must have laid her hands on me with as much delight and confidence as I now felt with Sam.

My father was beside himself. He brought a stuffed frog the size of three newborn infants and gloated at the baby's resemblance to himself. When we visited in Los Angeles, casually he did something inexplicable. Watching the baby wave his fat legs on a blanket on the backyard grass, he said to me suddenly, "You know, I bet you'd like to see some snapshots of yourself at his age." He stepped into the house and came out with a package full of photographs, each one a censored memory.

Oh, yes, there were baby pictures of me—of passing interest to a new mother, I suppose. But there she was, my own mother—unremembered, unmentionable, her memory suppressed, and all these photographs hidden for thirty years. I feasted my eyes. The wealth of detail contained in that envelope! As much as I could want! She was pretty and dressed with a flair in the style of the time—angular forties clothes, costume jewelry all spirals and clusters, a whole array of hairdos over many pictures that bespoke a strain of womanly experiment, maybe even vanity. In many of the snapshots, she mugged for the camera, joking . . . a sense of humor, a zaniness, was not something I had ever imagined. There was a series of shots of her setting the table for a modest little dinner party of friends—it was clearly before I was born; the figure she cut was certainly not that of a woman who had had a baby. I looked at the dishes, the hamburgers, the mismatched silverware and plastic cups, and a ketchup bottle in the center with the salt and pepper shakers, and saw that my parents at the start of their lives together had struggled with the demands of daily life as Tom and I were struggling now.

Yet such was the strength of my father's will, and his power over me on his own turf, that the censorious habits of thirty years remained irrevocably in place. We stood on the concrete patio, under the wooden-slat canopy, and oohed and ahhed over the image of myself as a naked infant, never mentioning, *never mentioning!* the animated, stylish, often lovely and sometimes beautiful young woman whose face and form in black and white filled every white-framed snapshot. Never had I stood more deeply in the shadow of the elephant than I did that afternoon, with my baby son waving his legs on the lawn.

For a long, long moment, I could have murdered my father for suppressing not only my memories but these photographs, these records of what she had been. But as he crowed at my baby's attempts to push himself over on his back—"That child has the strength of a six-month-old!" he cried proudly—forgiveness welled up, even gratitude. Better now than never, I told myself in the sun, and beneath awareness the frayed ends of a torn connection rebraided themselves in my soul.

Some weeks later, back home with Tom and Sam, and with the photographs put away in a special album, the last bit of reweaving took place. A cousin from that lost time surprised me with a call. He was a law professor, teaching for the summer at Stanford. In my first separation from Sam, I had lunch with him and his family while Tom stayed home with the baby. In a rush, involuntarily, I broke the taboo and asked if he remembered anything about my mother. No, but his mother would, he felt sure. Soon afterwards, I received a letter from her in which she identified herself as my mother's first cousin and close friend. My mother had come to a party at her house the day before she died, wrote my cousin. She had looked radiant; she was a wonderful woman, always laughed. My cousin still missed her.

Then the short letter got down to business: fifty years ago my new correspondent had been starting her career as a teacher. My grandfather, she told me, had been an insurance salesman and had sold her a policy. Now this insurance policy had matured; coincidentally her son had spoken of me. "I send this to you for your baby," the letter calmly informed me. "You can think of it as a gift from your grandfather." Slipped into the envelope was a check for $1,000.

I thought of it, instead, as a gift from my mother—a phantom who all my life had cast her own shadow but never appeared squarely in the open field of my imagination. And in a rented house on a wild Northern California hillside whose unfinished back wall was nothing but a piece of plastic rattling in the wind, and in a household created by two egalitarians, each with a commitment to a separate art whispering demands for attention, supplies, and *time,* the financial burdens of parenthood had us waking in the night and begging for mercy. That check fluttered out of its envelope like Noah's dove settling on the olive tree, signaling possibilities at the end of a long storm.

Mended, the floor of my soul was finally strong enough to bear my full weight. I stepped up on it as onto a swing. Tentatively at first, I began to write in earnest, swooping back and forth from deepest past to imagined future. Handing Sam back and forth into each other's care, through trial and error Tom and I invented ways to live as a family and do our chosen work. But I felt myself swinging just above a fork with three sharp prongs—motherhood, work, and art—always in danger of being skewered by one, two, or all three. To earn money, I doggedly copyedited manuscript after manuscript, here and there stealing time from myself to write a story. It was true that my silences had been long and hard and sometimes filled with bitterness. But as with a whole new generation of emerging writers—think of Tillie Olsen herself, *As I Stand Ironing,* think of the finally freed, richly timbred songs of Alice Walker, Isabel Allende, Toni Morrison—the voices I found in myself, when I found them, were those of daughter *and* mother. Within me I suddenly heard them, calling to each other and searching for ways to blend as they lifted themselves into song.

1. Tillie Olsen, *Silences* (New York: Delacorte, 1978), 31.

TEN

George Eliot's Birthday

True, I was flying high, but eventually the tine marked *livelihood* on that three-pronged fork brought me down.

There's a famous image in the literary folklore, of Harriet Beecher Stowe rocking a cradle with her foot as she wrote *Uncle Tom's Cabin* by candlelight. Maybe I had electric lights and a wind-up swing, but the manuscripts I slaved over the minute the baby's eyes sank closed or the second he was off at child care were the dearly loved work of other people. Book after book after book after book, I copy-edited, indexed, proofread, proof checked, evaluated, "styled up," and rewrote. No doubt WLP would have stuck his thumbs beneath his suspenders to indicate his pride, but to me the manuscripts were nothing but stumbling blocks, piled into a wall that separated me from the writer's life.

The work was dead hard. An unbelievable amount of virtually invisible work goes into transforming a manuscript into a book—even the author (sometimes *especially* the author) is unaware of the brainpower and sweat invested by others before the words are rendered into type.

Today I can turn to a paragraph in the startling book *The Wages of Writing* to find that there was a long precedent for the life of toil that was keeping me from my real work. Here's what the authors have to say about book writers in the eighteenth century:

> Sheer poverty compelled many of them to sell their souls to whomever would give them work—for political pamphlets, scandal sheets, pornography, the grind of ghosting and devilling, or any of the other chores associated with starvation scribbling. And it was poverty that gained them a reputation for minor crookery and evil living, cheating tradesmen, haunting whorehouses and drink shops, and dodging bailiffs and landlords.[1]

Had I been able to look up, perhaps I would have gotten smart and turned to crime. As it was, I sharpened my teeth on three or four book projects at once—big fat college textbooks from every field, from human sexuality to computer programming; trade books about everything from whale watching to rheumatism to reaching an alpha state by lying inside a circle of copper wire. I met every stringent deadline and learned how to run interference between hurt, crabby authors and harried, underpaid staff editors. At night I read problematic fiction manuscripts and wrote analyses for a fee.

The definite high point of this grueling stretch was the feverish few days in which, in response to a classified ad in the *Chronicle* calling for "adult" movie scripts, I hammered out a steamy screenplay on a medical theme (in my cover letter I called it "mediporn"). I sent it off under the name Maggie Powers and waited in vain for a check in the mail. Later I wondered how many other writers had gone for that scam as fervently as did, and I truly consider it possible—it was a *very* hot script—that in some sleazy theater with sticky floors Maggie Powers had her shining moment.

Tom was keeping the same pace in the printing trade—running an in-house printing operation by day, then putting the baby on his back for long after-dinner walks through the hills before disappearing into the darkroom until the morning hours. Who knows—maybe he was asleep in there. I certainly nodded off routinely over a mountainous computer manuscript or a textbook on population genetics.

It was work, it was definitely an education (analyzing fiction problems especially), and I at least wasn't beholden to a boss—I could fool myself into thinking I'd soon be doing my *real* work. But strive as we might, we came up short every month. If the work was hard, the money was hell. My friend Linda G., who is a single mother supporting herself and her young daughter as a freelance editor, told me once that she *welcomed* the insomnia that follows the night terrors about money. It gave her an opportunity to put in three or four uninterrupted hours on a manuscript. Now, *wait* a minute, Linda, as Jack Benny used to say.

When Sam was three, I saw a classified ad in a trade magazine: "Freelance editors wanted to gather and discuss professional matters." I flew to the phone and spent an hour immersed in that special heady mixture—one part network-ing to one part down-and-dirty professional gossip. The woman who had placed the ad was a freelancer with a child of nine, lots of business savvy, and no inconvenient writerly dreams to interfere with her peace of mind. But she also had a wealth of stories and hard-won lessons to discuss about the freelance life. Our excited conversation kept circling the same ever more obvious conclusion. Organize!

The first meeting of what came to be known as the Bay Area Freelance Editors' Guild was not inspiring. Quite the opposite—the gathered, myself included, looked like we'd been dragged and dropped by cats onto some-body's living room floor. The prevailing mood among the fifteen or so freelancers in the room seemed to be the kind of chronic depression often attributed to low self-esteem, but more fruitfully viewed as the inevitable result of over-work and underpay. Needless to say, we were all women.

The first several meetings were grueling since, though strangers to each other, we needed to achieve the level of candor necessary to identify the professional issues and conflicts that we shared. First among them was pay, of course, and nobody wanted to admit to the pitifully low wages she was staying up nights to pull in. Even worse was the possibility—later confirmed—that the same publishers were paying us different fees, straight-facedly agreeing to the ladylike figures we cited per project or per hour. At a subsequent meeting, we invited a managing editor from a local publishing firm—one that had employed us all as independent contractors over the years—to speak to us. He assumed the amused and indulgent tone men often use to impart wisdom to a roomful of women, and said, "You girls"—it was barely 1980—"now, you girls *never* charge up to budget. We figure a budget for each book, slot in an amount for outside editorial work, and then we ask you what you'd charge to provide it. Don't you ever hear us laughing as you walk out the door? You *never* even *approach* the budgeted figure."

Ha, ha.

We were, as a rule, well-educated, highly conscientious (to the point of obsessive perfectionism) bookworms with a lifelong love of language and a bred-in-the-bone abhorrence of discussing money. We could have been in business, but instead we were hanging onto the margins of the publishing industry by our bitten-down nails, laboring into the night and nervously ripping open the manuscript envelopes we had just sealed to review our work just one more time. We *did* suffer low self-esteem, because we earned so little money. And, alas, we earned so little money because we suffered from low self-esteem.

It was a hard lesson to learn, but we cheered each other on. We found ways to laugh at our lack of business craft and our general timidity in watching out for ourselves. At one of the early meetings, an editor who shared my literary aspirations gave me hysterics when she announced that she had had to cancel her subscription to *Coda,* a wonderful magazine now called *Poets and Writers,* because she began to read it the moment it arrived and it so overstimulated her imagination with writing fantasies and ideas that she lost a whole afternoon's worth of editing. We bemoaned the torture of being hired, as a copy editor at a copy editor's wages, to salvage an unspeakable mess of a manuscript. We all shared the horror of overbooking, and the unthinkable situation of having a whole season's work suddenly canceled when an author lost a job or got a divorce or suffered a block and failed to deliver a manuscript. Slowly our barriers went down, and by way of anonymous lists dropped into a hat, we managed to share our fee scales and sort out discrepancies. We identified issues. We set professional standards. We developed a decision-making protocol and created that nemesis, committees.

We held workshops and seminars and studied the effects of self-employment on self-esteem. Cautiously skirting federal restrictions against creating a monopoly, we attempted to standardize our rates and develop a code of business practices. We waxed nearly metaphysical in attempting to draw distinctions between copy editor, line editor, substance editor, developmental editor, rewriter, collaborator, and ghost. We swapped horror stories and died laughing. Then we set about identifying red flags in our business relationships and brainstorming for fair responses to them.

We created a handsome brochure setting forth the standards of our profession.

We voted ourselves a cost-of-living increase.

We perked up and began, as a group, to dress rather well.

But my enthusiasm flagged after a year, when—in my estimation—it was time to support each other into giving ourselves a cost-of-living raise. Eyes cut away, weight was gained, and a deadly belief—assumed to be eradicated—surfaced again: that working with books was recompense enough . . . who needed to become strident over money?

We had done an amazing job of bootstrapping, but we hit the glass ceiling with a crash. Once out of the group, I realized that the reluctance was well-rooted in reality. Pushing forward, we were in danger of pricing ourselves out of the market. There were hundreds, perhaps thousands of highly educated lady bookworms out there, to whom, without benefit of our shared effort of evolving a professional identity, $12.50 per hour sounded like just about what they dared to think they were worth (today's standard rate for freelancers in the publishing industry, *twelve years later,* is not much higher).

At the end of each madcap day, a haphazard patchwork of preschool, day care, editing, reviewing, shopping, cooking, coming and going, I looked deep inside myself for my commitment to writing serious fiction and found something dark and shriveled and rotten, something wasted and ruined, something that, if tasted, would surely be bitter enough to bring tears to the eyes.

I had a small sheaf of published reviews and stories, and a large file filled with promising drafts of more, but I was thirty-eight years old, far too old to be a beginner at anything.

It wasn't decorous to continue to crave artistic achievement. It wasn't practical; it wasn't realistic; it wasn't *motherly.* And yet I knew that the bitterness of Cassandra, which I had discovered within myself and which was already corroding my professional relationships and even tainting a friendship here and there, would grow to fill not just myself but my marriage and my relationship with my son.

In the end I resigned myself to my vain ambitions. I could not give them up, but I could pare them down to the bone. Forget writing short pieces, I told myself. Besides the discouraging diminishment of venues for fiction, the work of keeping submissions of short stories circulating added more paperwork to the sea that was pulling me down. And anyway, I was a ravenous reader of long fiction. The novel was my natural form. I determined to write a novel or quit for good.

But life being life, and the mind's greatest aspirations being as minnows to the body's desires, I found, to my unaccountable joy, that I was pregnant again.

George Eliot published her first book, *Scenes of Clerical Life,* at thirty-eight, and the thirty-ninth birthday, which I had just passed, was famous for planting despair in the discouraged breasts of women who "wanted to write." And yet there was still time. Thinking again of the bitterness I had been shocked to find within, I discovered in a George Eliot chronology that she had published her first *novel, Adam Bede,* at forty.

My determination was so fierce I managed to save enough money to give myself six months' worth of paid maternity leave. I set out on faith that fate would grant me two, only two, requirements: the facility to create a draft of my short novel before my savings ran out, and a healthy, peaceful baby who slept through the night and napped three and a half hours a day. Amazing to tell, given its usual fickleness, the universe complied.

1. Paul William Kingston and Jonathan R. Cole, *The Wages of Writing: per Word, per Piece, or Perhaps* (New York: Columbia Univ. Press, 1986), 11.

BLOOMING

ELEVEN

Noises

Waking up every morning at five to write fiction before the family gets up means laying down a dark strip of fantasy under the week. For me, a natural slugabed, getting up was horrible every day, especially in the cold and damp of winter. And waves of irritability plagued me in the early evenings. . . . But the deep silence, broken gradually by waking birds and the slow lifting of the darkness, the disappearance of my own reflection in the window of my little porch office, and the subtle revelation of the pasture and cows—these were secrets I barely realized I enjoyed as I stared deep into my computer screen, weaving my story and playing my keyboard as if it were a piano. The bitter nut of an unfulfilled future, like the pit of Cassandra's heart, melted away as my novel took shape, moved forward, accrued. And I knew that I was saved.

Like every writer, I had had to accept the hand I was dealt and play with it. That meant reentering rape, random urban violence, and the rage and hatred of strangers, of which I had had an all too detailed view. I challenged myself to create a story that would not only lead me to the heart of these realities, but also convey that essence to others in a way they could receive it. Strangely, I encountered no inner resistance, and instead found diving into memories long shunted aside to be a fluid, deeply satisfying experience. Perhaps it was all those years of brushing the meaning away—since the purpose of rape, humiliation, is its only meaning—that gave me something like relief at taking out those old, indelible memories in the dark, silent early morning hours. Dispassionately I sorted through them, turning them this way and that, the way you would some old bones, a feathered wing, the pelt of a long-dead animal—things once exquisitely sensitive but lifeless now.

And I had my baby, Evan. I even rocked him with my foot while I wrote. And I had my son, Sam, now five, and my husband, Tom. Once I heard Edna O'Brien, one of my most loved writers, in answer to a question at a reading, assert that it was impossible for a contented person, a person without inner turmoil, to be a writer. And I read one time that Richard Ford taught the would-be writers in his creative writing classes that if you wanted to be a writer, you couldn't have children: choose. But I think if I were asked to name what I needed to become a writer, I would have to say—proud feminist that I am—that I could only write well-loved. It took me until nearly forty to feel myself on solid ground, secure in my family. And in that context my memories of being targeted and hurt by angry men on the rampage were nothing to me anymore but ancient feathers and bones.

From the practical point of view, I found motherhood periodically noisy and demanding, but caring for children involves many stretches of long, empty time. Nursing, rocking, slowly turning the pages of picture books while eager eyes drink up every detail, dropping children off, picking them up, waiting for day care to be over, waiting for drawing lessons to be over, waiting for soccer practice, Little League, gymnastics, other kids' birthday parties to be over. Without diminishing the racketing irritation and anxiety, and without forgetting the terrible grit necessary to get up and write every morning before dawn, let me call in print to other mothers who despair over their art.

You can *think* in those times; you can work things out. Like a pregnant woman growing a child while she attends to other things, you can think out a story and ready it for the moment you steal for yourself. In keeping with Ernest Hemingway's advice in *A Movable Feast,* I always got up from my desk before I was finished for fear of having nothing to write when I next sat down to work again. I went episode by episode through my novel, and it was at the wheel of my car, or in the shower, or even as I read the wacky cadences of Dr. Seuss that the next scene, the next knot, the next inch or two of plot floated up.

In the fifties my father had a novelty item that he brought out at parties. It was a black plastic eight ball filled with liquid, and if you asked it a question and turned it over, a short silly answer slowly floated up into view. Every time that, here and there within the family chaos, I turned my mind to my book and suddenly saw where to go next, I thought of my father's eight ball. So fierce was my determination to snatch myself from the brink of waste that if I had to stand on my head to make the next scene float to the surface, then goddamit, I'd tuck my baby under my arm and stand on my head.

Terrified that I would see criticism or—the worst!—boredom in the quiver of an eyelash, I never told anyone what I was doing. Instead, in trepidation, I enrolled in a writer's workshop with novelist Alice Adams, and set the workshop as my deadline for finishing a draft of the book. It was ass-backwards, I suppose, to take the class *after* I wrote the book, but I knew that the spell I was under was self-hypnosis, initiated and fostered from within. It was a terror to apply, since I had to send a piece of current work. I knew that if I were rejected for the workshop, my new identity as a novelist—as vulnerable as a shell-less egg, its membranous surface trembling—would spill away forever.

The workshop was all women, each one as earnest as I. That do-or-die quality permeated the circle around the table, and I can still remember every story that was read. Giving voice, giving voice. A Latina woman read a story about the barrio. A sharp, stylish Berkeley woman wrote about smart, stylish, unforgiving women drinking next to a potted palm in an elegant hotel. One with the hint of a Scottish brogue wrote of the complex interplay of characters in a small Northern California town. A very shy writer, whose being has left no trace at all in my memory, read an unforgettable first-person monologue in the voice of a woman crazed by poverty.

I read a chapter from the middle of my novel—and shook.

Now, with experience, I know I always shake when work I read aloud has struck through to the truth, but that day I flapped and rattled like a Halloween skeleton, embarrassed. Still, from the first moment I could feel the attention of fifteen writers focus and catch—they were with me! When I finished I could hear the collective breathing go from shallow back to normal, and I knew I would be a writer. Kind words were said, as they had been for all the other stories, but these were extraneous. I had enrolled in the workshop for a secret purpose. In the very air of that college classroom, I felt what I had hoped without hoping to feel: I had touched them.

I came to find out that literary agents and editors at publishing houses were another can of worms entirely.

"Well-written, but so dark."

"Well-written, but depressing."

"Well-written, but . . . don't you have something more upbeat?"

"Well-written, but . . . "

There was a day, though, when an agent called me up and, in a New York accent as forceful as a subway, told me that my story of rape and pregnancy had kept her awake all night. Days later she sold it to a prestigious publisher. Weeks later an editor wrote me a letter gently suggesting certain revisions, which I made in a two-day, overstimulated writing binge. Months later I read the proof. One day, unheralded, one copy of *Coming Back Up* came in the mail.

I could have been in one of those upscale telephone commercials pandering to the artistic gentry. I resisted the temptation to knock on the houses all up and down my rural road to show off my book—perhaps unnecessarily undistinguished in appearance, if looked at now, objectively—to neighbors I had never met in all the time I'd lived there. Following that came a heady raft of readings, radio talks, even television interviews. Then came a spate of lovely reviews.

And then, with the sound of an unseen door slamming at the end of a very long corridor, nothing. It was over.

But if I had hoped to see my words in print before, now I had been bitten and infected with that unladylike disease, ambition. Never mind—the Brontës had had it, George Eliot had had it, Jane Austen had had it, even someone as seemingly prim as Barbara Pym had had it. Tillie Olsen had certainly had it, as did a million "mid-list" writers like me, whose stories, like mine, had quietly risen on a single swell in an ocean of books and then disappeared. And a good thing they all had it, too. Although cliché has it that writing is one part inspiration to nine parts sheer hard work, what cooks the pie is the heat of desire. Without that, says a voice in my head from the Old Country, all you got is apples.

But given the fact that my writing life was still a 5-to-7-A.M. affair, my single ambition remained modest: merely to stay in print. As soon as the manuscript of *Coming Back Up* had left my hands, I found another story—and was surprised and even a little miffed to discover that this one too focused on sexual violence. In *Out of Danger*, I wrote of the relationship between a mother and daughter after the girl has been snatched from the street and then, months later, returned. Her only medicine is love—you see how I drew from what I knew—yet the savaging leaves her with an inability to receive it.

My editor bought this story in partial form. Now I had the luxurious opportunity, as the sun rose every morning, to write a book I knew would see print. As before, only more fluidly, the story unrolled scene by scene, and I began to understand certain truths that I work by now:

- that one's creative process is as unique as one's fingerprints;

- that in practicing one's art, the writer explores and becomes acquainted with that process and finds ways to adapt it to life's contingencies—which means, when available time is short, writing short books;

- that the more writers understand their own process, the more fully they can trust it, the more profound is the pleasure, and the more mature the results.

Writers, it takes *years*.

Wannabes, dreamers, enrollees in creative writing work-shops, attendees at writers' conferences, sidewalk pounders and country walkers indulging your fantasies of fame and fortune! It takes *years* for us to understand what we can ac-complish and where our work can take us. And you can't reach it in a single book. Artistically speaking, of course. Regarding what we can accomplish career-wise, the whole publishing industry is trying its anxious best to determine the magic formula to that. Certain writers tap a vein right from the start, and the vein turns out to branch and con-nect, capillary to capillary, with readers everywhere. But those writers are the fortunate freaks, and they play in the same lottery we journeymen writers do.

Writing is a lifelong journey, a slow revealing and minute exploration. Once begun, there will be the stalls and grinding uphill pushes that any ride entails. But there will also be those inevitable glides—through terrains dark and frightening or flooded with sunlight, it doesn't mat-ter—that bring joy to the traveler and stoke the desire that fuels the creative engine.

With my second novel headed for publication, I was on a long, whooping glide and filled with joy and desire. But out of nowhere came the only thing that could stop me, and suddenly I saw that it was possible that I might die on that clattering train.

TWELVE

Mysteries

Yesterday morning and today I have been walking, walking, walking the rural roads through the countryside, struggling. The fog from the coast rolled back all around me as I stomped along, revealing the soft, rolling Sonoma prospects, all the more glorious for being deeply familiar. Still, I could barely look up and see the morning take shape, so intense was my internal struggle, suddenly, with self-consciousness about my book. My work as a novelist has been to *escape* tyrannical reality, to push back its limitations on imagination, to *make things up*. But here I was every day telling my life—and who the hell was I? Worst of all, if I were really going to explore the growth of my writer's identity, I had to revisit cancer, dismantle the official version that I had told myself and probe it too for meaning.

On the other hand, I countered, compared to making up fiction, a factual story unfolds with such wonderful *ease*. That's one way to look at it, I realized: my life as first draft.

I laughed here, walking alone in my sun hat, the mumbling, grumbling writer who passes by her neighbors' windows arguing with herself.

The issue remained unresolved, but later in town, when I broke for coffee at the little Armenian cafe, a friend leaned over as he passed my table. "Do you know who that is?" he asked me in a stage whisper, indicating a man in a wheelchair in a crisp white shirt.

"No, who?"

"That's Ron Kovic, who wrote *Born on the Fourth of July.*"

It took my breath away. I'd been *thinking* about Ron Kovic. My belief in the random universe was seriously shaken. I had read Kovic's memoir of his return from Vietnam, paralyzed by a spinal injury, in 1976, long before it was a movie. Through his personal story the war and its consequences sprang alive for me with a new level of particularity. Had I even *once* considered him self-indulgent for plumbing for meaning in print the horrendous injuries that interrupted his youth and changed the course of his life? Far from it—the opposite was true. His scrupulous effort to name, scrutinize, and reflect on every aspect of his trauma—from emotional to sexual to intellectual to political—had inflamed me anew with a commitment to the truth and to finding the meaning underlying experience. And, by example, it taught an old lesson again: that books, far more than face-to-face relationships, are the doorways into other people's lives.

Now, here in our sleepy little Northern California river city was Ron Kovic himself. His book had recently been translated by Oliver Stone into a movie that walloped my whole generation, grown soft in middle age, into remembering the Vietnam war and beginning to see over the distance of time what it had done to us all. I fumbled around, glad he was deep in conversation, trying to figure out what to do. Not a celebrity collector, and certainly not into autographs, I finally decided to write him a note on the back of a business card.

"Read it to me," he said, waving away my miniature missive. "I forgot my glasses."

"Oh, I'll just leave it with you. I only wanted to thank you for writing your story and tell you I've been thinking of you." He slipped the note into his wallet and seemed to understand the familiarity coming from a perfect stranger. Perhaps he was used to it.

"Give me a hug," he demanded, in a cousinly way.

So, writer to writer, over coffee, I embraced him in his chair, pressing my temple to his and secretly attempting to draw the courage I needed to tell the story of my darkest hours.

Some messages require no words. My son knew his beloved dog had died by the quality of our pause, on both extensions, when we called him at camp. I knew I had cancer by the sudden officiousness of the X-ray technicians at the mammogram clinic. Where minutes before we had been rolling along in lively conversation, during the reshoot following the film check, they had ducked into a remoteness I would come to recognize. It was the safe house, filled with busy work and workaday distractions, of all medical messengers with bad news to tell.

No words were exchanged, but I was sure. Nevertheless, gripping the wheel to quit my hands' shaking and singing with the radio to drown out the sound of my own breathing, I drove to Berkeley to hear Grace Paley read her poetry and her "short short pieces," and I felt that there was nothing else I could have done that night. A soft, rounded woman wearing a heavy sweater over her shoulders like a shawl, she presented small morsels of fiction wrapped in starchy humor—comfort food, like the Jewish stuffed noodles called kreplach—and it was all I could do to keep from flying down to the podium and hurling myself into her motherly arms.

Next morning I sat in my porch office in my father's old office chair, the closest I could get to him since his death five years earlier. I watched the light come up outside on the pasture where the cows came down to graze in the dawn hours. It was February, the first rains had raised dense green grass, and even before I saw the cows I could hear their feet meeting the solid earth and their thick square teeth tearing the grass from the ground.

The doctor's confirming call laid a new reality upon our multilayered life—cancer, which consists of occasional crises strung together by long waiting periods of slowly sinking fear. Work saved me. My editorial plate was over full, and I had begun a novel called *Runaway*, about the long-dead mother of teenage twins who turns out to be alive. On Valentine's Day 1987, I had a biopsy. Late in February, on the anniversary of my father's death, I would have to have the breast removed.

It disturbs me, when I read a book, to be suddenly tripped into a new point of view—from first person into third, or vice versa. But I've noticed that fear for your life tends to encourage a shift into third person, or at least a desperate impulse toward it. One more grand cliché began to drive our family life with my diagnosis and the terrible immersion in the medical culture: that the greatest fear is fear itself. Fear was a rank-smelling, panting animal that sat on my chest and constricted my breathing and my view. From that vantage point, it filled our house and my family's hearts with the fumes of its terrible breath. I can only speak for myself when I say that the best I could do was inch my way out from under its awful weight and watch from a distance. In that sense assuming the third person allowed me some intermittent relief, and I assume it here only briefly to convey that feeling of watching.

For the past four Sundays, on a trip north, the woman had gone to the aquarium late in the afternoon, paid her money, and waited for the crowd to empty out in the underground viewing chamber. It sounded and smelled so particularly *human* in the commotion of winter raingear— the necks, the hands, the lips, the matted heads to uncover upon entering, to cover back up on leaving. Gradually, as she willed herself to be patient, the families, the tourists, the tired hungry babies, would climb the stairs and melt away. Then she would have the view of the whales to herself.

There were two belugas, natives to the coast, both females. Among the smallest of whales, they were perhaps twice the size of dolphins. One was gray—the young ones were gray, she had learned from the presentation the first time she had come. One was white, a luscious, creamy white that somehow emphasized the solidity of the muscle beneath the skin. The whales turned white as they aged, the young presenter had explained in the frigid, concrete amphitheater upstairs surrounding the beluga pool. It was that that drew her somehow—the slow, slow, decades-slow whitening of the whale.

They had the dolphin's smile and funny egghead skulls—their heads and faces seemed designed to amuse. The heads had interested her little until she had seen the calm acceptance in the eyes. But the smooth arcs of bodies as the pair moved through the jade-green water—they captivated the woman like music and calmed her racing mind.

She was ill. The surgeons were going to cut her. She had twelve more days before they did their work, and it felt like the final assault upon her womanhood.

And she had just begun to understand how love and loving worked! Many times a day as she went about in her life now, she could, were she to give in to the urge, simply stop and cry up to the sky. She had just begun to understand! She had just begun to see—so late!—beauty and meaning in herself as a woman and to comprehend the language of the body. And in twelve days they would take from her quite matter-of-factly the symbol of the system that she finally saw was love.

The two whales swam slowly together. Then they each split off from their tandem way and exercised alone. The white one played with a weighted inner tube, wearing it on the curved dome of her head, the silly smile made self-satisfied by its jaunty tilt. There was no doubt at all that the whales watched the people. Was this playful one imitating those among the viewers who wrapped their heads carefully before entering their own element up the stairs?

This visit was a good one. The viewing chamber emptied out twenty minutes before closing time. The woman had the bench to herself as she watched the belugas swimming. And it occurred to her suddenly that they would be here in the dark—that every night, they were swimming or hanging in the dark. The thought scared her more deeply than she had known she could feel, and she sat motionless to let the awful fear pass.

She would float up through the darkness of the anesthesia, she would feel sleep lift from her tail. She would move only a little, only minutely, to spin slowly upward in the water toward the dawning morning light. The sleek smoothness of her white body—perhaps it would give her pleasure as she moved, oh so minutely, through the water. She would be a glowing crescent of thick, shadowed muscle and invisible articulated bone. She would suddenly see the dark shadow of her young and supple sister.

"Beluga," said the woman aloud as the calm, white, silent creature, gazing, drifted by. "Beluga," she said again, taking the word as a mantra.

Once on the surface again, having swum up through the thick, sick jelly of anesthesia to sink down time and again before emerging, I found I had been wrong and there was love abundant. Tom's first response to my altered body, delivered in his dry, off-the-cuff style when I showed him the stapled incision, set me at ease on that score, perhaps for the rest of my life. After he crossed his arms, looked without flinching, contemplated for a moment, what he said was—an inspired lie—"I like it. It's punk."

Saved again.

"But what can you live without?" asked Evan, my younger son. He was four years old, and I knew exactly what he meant. Sam, just entering preadolescence, didn't want to talk about the medical realities that had befallen our household, but Evan was avid. Lying side by side in the dark in his narrow bed, together we went through the nonessential body parts—digits first, limbs, teeth, eyeballs, ears.

Cautiously, he wondered, "Breasts?"

Oh, certainly. Not necessary in the least, especially since the need to nurse children was long in the past now. As for looks—well. Well.

"But"—impatiently—"Stomachs?" Nope.

"Lungs?" You could do with one.

"Kidneys?" Oh, yes. One friend managed very well with no kidneys. He cleaned his blood himself.

But Evan was getting exasperated. "I mean, what *can't* you live without?"

"You know, Ev, even if you die you keep living as long as somebody remembers you."

The words jumped out of my mouth in the darkness and set my course for the next three years.

My child fell asleep in the sudden, surprising way tired children do, and I stared at the ceiling and narrowed my eyes at the memory of my father's image. I remembered how I'd tortured him for memories of my mother during the last year of his life. By then he wasn't unwilling but— "It's thirty-five years, Shug," he'd reminded me, staring at the blank television screen. Now she had been forty years unmentioned, forty years, eliciting nothing but agitation. Forty years locked away from the mainstream of life, put underground and abandoned.

I was four when she died, and now my own youngest child, this Evan, was four. When that coincidence occurred to me, a new fear blew up from within like a howling wind. I had almost convinced myself that losing a piece of myself as I had was like the loss by a healthy, hearty tree of a blighted branch. But now I trembled at the possibility: I would die and, repeating my history, my child would forget me and I would be gone.

It was existential terror so far beyond tears that I had to creep away from the bed and step outside into the wide country night. The giant eucalyptuses along the creek bed in front of our house were swaying in the wind, filling the country silence with ocean sounds, and my fear radiated out into the starry black sky the way the heat of the day rises off the earth—while the creatures of the hemisphere sleep.

For forty years the shadow of the elephant had hidden my mother from me, and so dark was the ground within its boundaries that even after he died and his will to suppress was gone, the ground remained infertile, dead. How, *why* did he do that to me? How could he have done that to her?

Mysteries, before me and behind.

I was unaware then, but in that moment of hyperconsciousness next to Evan in the dark, the heart had gone out of my book in progress, *Runaway.* Though I continued to work hard on it, it was a child's book, the fairy-tale fantasy about a mother's return to the children she had abandoned, and to my great disappointment none of the few people who read it liked it at all. What the story lacked was the intense, never-ending drama of life itself—the suspense that stemmed from the cold regularity of time, the infinite complexity of human motivation, and the ever-present mystery of death.

Still, it took me three years to give up that book. And I saw, a little, as I worked, that in my drumming need to write I was laying down prints. In my child's bed that night, I had begun to discern them: like tracks made in the snow, first by one animal, then by another, there were two sets jumbled together, mine and my mother's. The work of my life was to distinguish one set of tracks from the other before they all melted away without a trace.

FRUITION

THIRTEEN

Some Answers

The style of the house we live in is called California bungalow. The place is really just a gray box with white trim and a porch on the front; it's set far back from a long, lazy rural road four miles out of town. There's a creek down in front that runs under the road—Blue Jay Creek, if you can stand the cutesy tone. Around the creek bed, huge old eucalyptuses cluster and groan. In the wind, which rises up most afternoons in the summer, their foliage sways like heavy skirts, sometimes to a frenzy. Every once in a while, somebody reminds us that their roots are wide, not deep, and that they are liable to topple over onto the house.

The porch faces north, and then comes my little glassed-in office, where I have written many a book and gazed out at the grazing cows. I had often wondered why, years ago, when our landlords first drove to the house with us following them in our car, they went the long way around from town. But it struck me once coming home from a walk: at a certain point the view is perfect. Fourteen acres of pasture-land surround the house, and behind is the long, soft sweep of the Sonoma landscape, famous for its rolling hills—which are mostly yellow, except for a short stretch in spring when they are emerald green—and clusters of oaks. Taking a long view from up the road, you can see the house as a boat in the safe harbor of the landscape, as wide and changing under the sky as the sea.

Such was the enduring nature of the home—true it was rented, but what home isn't transitory?—in which Tom and I and the boys were piecing together a family life one project at a time. Tom was by now a photographer full-time and I was editing, ghosting, and doggedly attempting to breathe more life into *Runaway*, while my first two novels invented new definitions for the term *modest sales*. Out there in the country, the telephone and mailbox were more than links, they were the central nodes in my social and business networks. And one day, down by the road and en-circled as my house was by the silent yellow hills, I with-drew from my mailbox the first answers to my forty-year mysteries. It was a delicious reversal on the ordinary belief, which holds that novelists mine their pasts for their stories. It turned out that my own small novels out in the world were about to restore my past.

Dear Suzanne,
As the self-appointed representative of your first-cousin-once-removed club, I congratulate you on your two recent books. My wife, Maggie, and I read them over the weekend.

There was never any doubt of the talent in your family—only where it would break out.

Your grandmother, my aunt, had the greatest sense of humor in the family in spite of the unspeakable tragedies she went through. She deserves you.

Should you visit our city, I assure you and your family a warm welcome.

Your cousin, M——

It was written on a lawyer's letterhead and signed by a man I'd never heard of. I conjured up the sad, gray image of my grandmother, who had lived downstairs from my father and me when my mother died. *The greatest sense of humor in the family . . .* And I remember only a mute old woman who had seemed weighted down by the heavy plaits of gray-shot brown hair twined around her head.

The unspeakable tragedies she went through. Unspeakable trage*dies*? What else had happened? Had she lost people to the Holocaust? Her name seemed German-Jewish—had she actually been a refugee? As the Holocaust literature had revealed, many American Jews of my generation met a wall of silence when probing for their family's experiences during the horror of those years. And often survivors were the most silent of all—what, *what* had happened to make her the mute, angry presence whose very sighs, in lieu of words, filled the flat downstairs with a sense of doom?

Of course, I wrote back instantly, effusively. Please, I said. Tell more, tell details, tell *anything*.

Even before receiving a reply from my newfound cousin, whom I calculated to be in his seventies, I received another letter:

Dear Suzanne,

I was a first cousin to your mother. That makes us first cousins once removed. My mother and your grandmother were sisters. Our families were very close.

It's amazing how I came to hear about you all over again. It was through your aunt [my stepmother's sister]. We met and liked each other and she lent me your two books . . .

My daughter and you were girlfriends when you were about two. Your mother died around April 11, 1948. Details after that are vague. I never met your stepmother, but I did see you again when you were sixteen years old. We even got you a date.

So you see I know quite a bit about you. One thing I will never forget. Before dinner that night, we sat down to talk. I mentioned your mother's sister, who died when she was thirty-one, and her brother, the youngest of the children, who died in the service. Your father had never mentioned them to you and I felt absolutely terrible that I was the one to bring you that news.

Your photo on the cover looks so much like your mother. You appear to be built like her too. I could go on but I won't.

My very best wishes.

There are facts you learn that simply do not fit reality. And once you come upon them and know they are true, you know too in a flash, as I did by my mailbox, that even personal reality is a constructed thing, a joint creation agreed upon, however uneasily, by your parents and yourself. So determined had my father been to protect me from the sad truth—that three of my grandmother's four children had died suddenly, unexpectedly, in a cluster in their thirties when I was in my very earliest years—that even when someone *told* me about the others, his prohibitions prevailed, and even when I had reached sixteen the facts had failed to take hold. I had no memory of this dinner or of my cousin's revelation about the very existence of an aunt and uncle who died tragic deaths. Some years later I met this cousin, and she told me that my father, upon learning of her innocent reference to my mother's siblings, never spoke to her again.

"I could go on but I won't."!

These poor, unsuspecting cousins! Little did they realize what they were getting into by writing to a writer and tantalizing her with the story of her life. I wrote back breathlessly, and no creative writing class was ever hounded more strenuously for details, details, *details.* By letter I was a terrier on their ankles.

My first correspondent wrote back again. I was disappointed to find a spare, page-and-a-half letter on the same formal legal letterhead. But the efficient, dictated style managed to convey many, many pieces of the puzzle:

> Dear Suzanne,
>
> The following is your family tree:
>
> [He then had typed in the names of my great-grandparents, Juda and Goldie, and the names of their seven children, one of whom was my grandmother. I am making the effort to honor the family privacy by not

revealing the names of the living. But, to restore them to the record of memory, I use the names of the dead.]

They came to this country in two groups, in the 1880s and 1890s. They originated in the eastern part of Latvia near the border of Latvia and Lithuania, which were then part of Russia.

In 1959, when Russia was opened to tourists, I applied for and was granted permission to travel to Russia. It was necessary to give a detailed itinerary to the Russian tourist office, before leaving this country. I told them the principal purpose of my trip was to rent a car in Riga, the port of entry to Latvia, and drive through the country visiting some of the towns that I had heard of during my childhood. I was assured there would be no problem, but when I got there, I was told that tourists were not allowed to travel outside Riga. My protest to the American ambassador got me nowhere. They assuaged my feelings by showing me Riga, taking me to dinner in a nice restaurant, where a miniature American flag was placed on my table and the orchestra played "Home on the Range."

Who *was* this man, I laughed to myself as I read this marvelous anecdote. I saw from the family tree that he had grown up in Elmira, New York, the home of Mark Twain's Clara and site of the Clemens's first home. Could it be something in the water that made one a teller of tales?

What followed were brief references—the barest outlines—of my mother's family:

Your mother, Elynore, died during childbirth (the baby also) when you were about 4.

Your Aunt Goldie died after a brief illness, I think in 1940.

Your Aunt Sylvia [this was the tall, shy, artistic aunt who lived downstairs with her husband and my grandmother and who helped my father care for me after my mother died] died of breast cancer when she was 53 or thereabouts. [Terror streaked through me at this, and though I was out in the open air a clock began ticking.]

The enclosed will tell you about your Uncle Paul.

Moving from clue to clue, I unfolded a formal missive on U.S. army letterhead. In the starkest sentence or two, it stated that Paul, while in the service in Panama, had taken his own life by asphyxiation.

So I was getting details, but nothing like those I had hoped for and expected. All these years I had longed for an assemblage of facts and subtle nuances that would suddenly gel into an *experience* of interacting with my mother. That no-doubt primitive, perhaps even biological, need had focused my attention too close, and never in all the years of wondering did I ever, ever wonder about her family. Perhaps that notable lack of curiosity was indeed a measure of my father's power as a censor of reality, but it made me feel foolishly self-centered and blindered to realize that even when the story had been handed to me at dinner, I had shunned it as irrelevant to the pale phantom I was pursuing.

It took me many weeks of returning to these facts on many country walks to understand and begin to sense my father's place, and then my own, in this tragic constellation. A phone call to my lawyer cousin, the M_____ of the letter, revealed that my father, then a young man of about twenty-eight, deemed himself the bearer to my grandmother of the news of my Uncle Paul's death. All of these terrible deaths, sudden and unexpected, clustered together in my earliest years, before my conscious memory began to function.

Perhaps, after all, I had had to become a parent to understand. But with the walking and thinking, walking and thinking, my father's motives in keeping these things from me became clear. Protectiveness is too mild a word in the face of such a tidal wave of grief. I think he knew intuitively, long before psychology became commonplace in everyday thought, that with respect to such brutal realities, a child as young as I was then was in danger of being swamped. I think this young man in his late twenties, already struggling financially, who had entered a doomed family out of love and who had taken his responsibilities as a family man with deadly seriousness, created to the best of his considerable ability a zone of safety for me and then defended it with the fierceness of two wild animals, both mother and father. The very beginnings of my memory tell me that this is true, and indeed it *was* safe and secure within the shadow of the elephant. I fought him back over the years to keep from being overwhelmed, but he never lost his anxious impulse to help keep me safe and untroubled—as if that were ever possible for anyone!—so I could flourish.

There was no great moment of insight or thunderous uprushing of the truth. It was just that I could look up from the road on my walks and see the rolling vistas that spread out around me. Now I even understood how he could have kept from me for thirty years all those photographs of my mother. And in understanding came a sharper recall of that protective fatherliness that I couldn't bring myself to malign even in my most straightforward and righteous assertions of feminist consciousness. Not a moment too soon, and across the terrible barrier of time, a hundred happy memories of him came rushing into my mind, and my love and gratitude flowed freely to my father.

Mushrooms in the dark, those hidden memories growing in the warm, fertile dampness of imagination behind doors slammed long ago. Not only were there more of them than I had ever sensed, but in their profusion they formed a story. Perhaps as I walked one of those doors swung open a bit, but a barrier remained.

It was fearsome facing down the last obstacle. It was something I could never have chosen to do. And yet what happened next jarred the last barrier aside and the story was released—not into memory but, transformed, into a book. I neither willed nor controlled the process, and once more I must admit that a full year passed before I recognized it for what it was—automatic writing, straight from the source. All I had to do—about all I *could* do—was put my hands on the keyboard and play.

FOURTEEN

No

"This pain is going to kill me," I told Tom. I was walking hunched over like an old lady. I was thin and gray and my stomach stuck out like a malnourished baby's. Everywhere I looked in the papers I saw reviews of Gilda Radner's book, *It's Always Something,* her cancer story, which had been published after her death. Every time I saw anything about the book, I averted my eyes. Gilda had been diagnosed with ovarian cancer when I had my mastectomy. Now, three years later, she was gone and I was trying to believe I was cancer-free. But every time, like a mosquito flying away from a hot frying pan, I flew away from an article on Gilda, I seemed to pick up another detail I didn't want to know. Finally, sick as a dog, I hobbled to an internist.

"I've got Gilda's symptoms," I made myself whisper.

"Now, now, dear," said he.

I've since learned the truth: doctors have as much denial about cancer as anybody else. It took them six months to hear me, to hand me off, from one specialist to another, to work through their various theories about urinary tract infections, irritable bowel syndrome, gynecological irregularities, menopause, and of course that well-worn sexist catch-all diagnosis, S-T-R-E-S-S. I came to find out, when I joined a support group for people with life-threatening diseases, that where cancer was concerned, misdiagnosis was the rule, not the exception. One of my fellow members, dealing with advanced brain cancer, had seen a long string of doctors about her headaches. The last one, a psychiatrist, had taken this woman's face in both hands and said, "Look at me, believe me. You're *not* sick. It's all in your mind!"

My months of uncertainty were like hell—I had children to raise, a living to make, books to edit, deadlines to meet, and a career as a novelist at a critical point.

And I had pain.

Forget cancer. I felt through it all I could easily die of fear.

The day came when I reached the right doctor, who looked at me with intelligent eyes, and spoke in a tone that conveyed his assumption that I could understand what he had to tell me. Once more, Tom and I sat through the words together, and I swear that it was only a technicality that the words applied to me rather than to us both.

"I'm pretty sure you have cancer again," the doctor said evenly. "The only question I have is what kind. Is it a recurrence of the breast cancer or a whole new cancer, probably of the ovaries? The scans we've done show enlargement of the ovaries, but frankly they're confusing. Not conclusive at all. We're going to have to go inside and take a look."

As in a dream, I simply got up and floated away—literally. I found myself in the hallway, having removed myself from the consultation room before I heard more than I could bear.

It was a horrendous surgery, and when I swam up this time, I knew without asking Tom that the news was not good. Days later, my doctor came in with another specialist to talk. "It is a very, very unusual presentation," he told me, "but we think it's the breast cancer that has metastasized to the abdomen. I removed as much as I could but . . . " Even this doctor had his unsayables. "But still—" he finally continued, as if hitting on something to say, "we can hope for a long remission."

We received the message in silence.

The second doctor, a man of my age bursting with vitality and good health, introduced himself and revealed a generosity of spirit in what he said that won my trust immediately. "I can't imagine what it must be like to hear what we have had to tell you. But you look to me so full of life that I can hardly believe you've been through a major surgery." We shook hands and they left.

There was nothing to say. Unusually for Tom and me, there was literally nothing to say.

At some point Tom left, temporarily, for a meal. A technician came in to fine-tune my television set. The maid came in to change the sheets. A nurse came in to adjust my morphine pump. My Mexican roommate's gigantic family formed a circle three-deep around her bed—and a second nurse came in to tell me my request for an egg-crate mattress to ease my back had been denied. This was the major surgery ward, where people were recuperating from all manner of unimaginable procedures. My room was next to the four at the end of the hall reserved for AIDS patients. The sounds drifting in from the corridor, especially at night, beg never to be described. "Sorry, no egg-crate mattress. You're just not sick enough," said the nurse.

At her words old outrages and new solidified within me into a spear. How like a rape mastectomy was—not only did they touch you, they took a piece of you away. You could only be grateful they didn't kill you in your sleep. How like a rape was surgery—they'd taken even more, and then come to stand beside your bed and comment on your staying power. How cruel this ironic evolutionary fluke— once you're past your childbearing years, your very hormones begin to poison you—literally—to death. The spear, long, straight, shiny, and hard as a diamond, flew from deep in my severed gut up through my throat and out my mouth. *"No!"* I cried, and the crowd froze. *"No! You can't tell me I'm not sick enough. I want that mattress and I've earned it and I won't shut up until I've got it!"*

Innocently, unaware of the turmoil, the young anesthesiologist who had been at my surgery entered the already packed room. "Did you know you came out of the anesthesia swinging? I don't suppose you remember, but you almost broke my nose," he told me.

"You get the fuck out of here!!!" I hollered at him like a witch, a crazy *bruja*. Out of the corner of my eye, I saw my roommate and her family cringe—none of them spoke

English, but they understood what I had said to this young White Coat. I was far, far gone, and finally the tears did come. Old tears, new tears, a terrible, humiliating, exhilarating, cleansing torrent of tears that seemed never to end, while the kindly television man at the end of my bed—he had, no doubt, seen many such dramas—continued working on the set. My roommate's family closed their mouths and closed their circle around the bed, the nurse proved merciful after all and came in to say she'd found me a mattress, and the Filipino maid with downcast eyes—who had told me that morning how she had left her children with her parents in the islands years ago—mopped the floor.

Later that night, when Tom had gone home, I found that books and television had been rendered unintelligible, as if in a foreign language, by my latest medical circumstances. But as I lay there wondering how I would get through the night, the muted clatter and bustle out in the corridor was overtaken by the sound of angels.

I do not overstate.

Harmony—sweet, tight, and richly complex. It was Christmastime. Carolers had come. It was the San Francisco Gay Men's Chorus. They worked their way slowly down the hall. At each room they stopped and sang two or three songs, sometimes more. They gave perhaps the only gift each of us in the rooms of that hall could receive that night—you didn't have to open it, you could have it in your bed, and it entered the head and sank down to the heart, like hope.

FIFTEEN

Recovery

If you have to have surgery, have it in the dead of winter. That way, by the time your strength is returning, it will be spring.

There's an outbuilding behind our house used by the landlords for storage. They call it the Granary, and it has a primitive porch in front of a sliding barn door that's just the perfect level for sitting. Every day after Tom and whoever of the many who helped us got the kids off to school, I'd go out there and sit on a pillow in the sun. After a while, motionless as I was, the birds would stop noticing me and swoop down close, insects and butterflies ignored me, the cattle grazing nearby didn't even see me, deer with their spotted fawns crossed the yard. It was the closest I'd ever come to feeling like Snow White.

But within I was facing a showdown. Things were different now, permanently changed for me. Soaking in my new relationship with the universe the way I soaked up the rays of the early spring sunshine, I was moving closer and closer to facing the fact that I could spend no more time on *Runaway*—that two and a half years was more than enough, and the manuscript still had problems. Jettisoning the book was difficult, very difficult. But I tried to comfort myself with my knowledge as an editor that every *real* writer has such a manuscript on her shelf, a misfit that never happened, a well-conceived story that failed.

Still, a more difficult question remained: if not *Runaway*, what? I might have no time to ripen slowly into maturity as a writer, and yet my desire to sing in my own voice was greater than ever. Given that my children were unmistakably happy and healthy, nothing in the world seemed more important than finding and raising that authentic voice and discovering what I could do with it. My first two novels, though praised and solid, were very strong beginning efforts, but beginning efforts nevertheless. In the literary derby, only the great exceptions seem to burst forth from the gate in their first race having found their stride and shown their full potential.

To practice while I wrestled, I finished a story I had begun before my surgery. It was the story of a teenage painter who didn't yet know that her painful vulnerability made her the true artist she was. But her pain was such, as an adolescent, that it killed her before she flowered—she drowned in a swimming pool. I set the story in the San Fernando Valley, where I had grown up, and it came out as smoothly as a skein of silk unwinding. It then occurred to me that I could tell the stories of all the characters who appeared in this first story, and one after another I did that. And quickly, smoothly, with no false starts, a family came into being—four children and a father, their family, lovers, neighbors, friends and enemies, and a teacher who had known them once.

There was no mother. Where was the mother? Surprise! The father had suppressed the mother's story. No one, not even the children, dared to ask where she was. Only an outsider, a housekeeper, gave voice to the mystery. "You got a ghost in this house, Mr. Jacobs," was how she put it.

One day, in a moment, the secret was revealed to me— one second at the kitchen sink I had no idea what had happened to the mother in this family, the next second I set a washed glass on the drainboard and I had the mother, whole. Her story became the prologue to *Remember Me.*

I have talked with many, many people with cancer, HIV infection, and other life-threatening diseases, and all experience a kaleidoscope of fear and anger and a sense of impending chaos. But there can be stretches, long stretches, of gratitude for the life after such a diagnosis. And there is an opportunity like no other to find out and enjoy who loves you and whom you love. But certain of us are blessed, temporarily anyway, with a mad, creative ecstasy in which all impediments fly away and the inner voice calls from the very bottom of the well. Each of these stories came up from the depths fast and whole, shot through with whatever beauty I was capable of rendering. It was a prolonged experience of art from the inside, and it brought with it a taste of where I could go if I were allowed the time.

Effortlessly, via a close friend, *Remember Me* found a publisher and became, in the production stages, a collaboration of book friends. I began to resume my domestic and editorial roles, and one day, driving through the back roads from Marin to Sonoma, I fantasized about a spring book party in what is called the fragrance garden of a rose farm near my home, one of my favorite places—and literary to boot, its designers having gained inspiration from the garden of Vita Sackville-West. Driving the looping country road, I thought about chocolate and strawberries. I pictured myself in fabulous blue clothes. And out there, with the clean air beating in, I shouted out loud. I'd been planning what to *wear* at a party nearly a year away! The future, which I hadn't yet dared to claim, came rushing back to surround me like a river crashing a dam.

Only one doubt plagued me during the production process of *Remember Me*—there were *two* deaths at the center of this book, that of the teenage artist and of Nancy, the mother, who has died a decade before the action of the novel begins. But not only were these deaths, they were suicides, and the book was very small. I feared they were too heavy, too much. "But these things happen," I tried to tell myself. "Children *do* learn suicide from their parents as a means of escape."

"The fact that it happens holds no weight at all. This isn't journalism," argued the internal editor. No one else objected, but I butted my head against the problem, trying to figure a way out. No go. These were the facts of this family's life, period. Much as I tried to alter their fates, these characters had come to me whole, with their lives lived out. I simply could not change the fundamental structure of their shared reality.

The book was launched at the fragrance garden in a gala, life-affirming party that was as close as is possible to the one I had envisioned on that country drive. As I hoped it would, the book took on a life of its own, and every now and then the look in a reader's eye or the timbre of voice tells me what I knew even at the time. Cancer had taken me in both horrid claws and dangled me over the abyss, but somehow or other that unknowable crone had brought me back and stood me on my feet—and in the process, in some mysterious way, I had finally become a true writer.

SIXTEEN

The Final Piece

Reader, you will not believe me.

With Sam, I traveled to Los Angeles for a writer's conference. I met two friends there who didn't know each other,
but, come to think of it, I mused, they resembled each
other in some ways. We were three Jewish women in our
middle forties. Within ten minutes it was revealed that both
my friends' grandfathers had taken their own lives during
the Depression. Amazing! I thought. But I was even more
taken with their candor than with the coincidence.

Next day I spent an enjoyable Sunday at a family
brunch, and I mentioned the incident.

"Oh, yeah, sure," said my uncle casually. This was my
stepmother's brother. They all came from the same small
eastern city we had left when we moved to California—in a
mind-numbing instant, he revealed that the family secrets I
had been collecting so painstakingly had been the stuff of
back-fence gossip. "Well, it's just like *your* grandfather." As if
we'd been discussing it on and off forever. As if I'd ever *heard*.

"What on earth—?"

"Well, you know. The Depression. It was common—suicide. He did it because . . . who knows? Business, I suppose. I never knew him."

I was speechless.

"Terrible for your mother, though. I knew her after that—she was in my class. She came home from high school and found him. She seemed to snap out of it, though. Great sense of humor, that girl. When I knew her. Oh, we laughed, I'm telling *you*."

Everything I'd written in my novel—the family with four children, the two suicides, one a parent, one a child; the theme of buried secrets and the obligation to bear witness to the lives of the dead. Certainly there had been gender changes, certainly artifice and tranformation by imagination. But the fundamental structure of my novel and its most central themes were rooted in fact. With the casual reference to the remaining piece in my family puzzle, I finally saw it all laid out page by page in my small book. Across the borders of time and even of death, each of the forgotten members of my family had called out to me and through me, and I had captured their messages in a title I had struggled hard to get right: "Remember me." And I'd really thought—though you may not believe it—I honestly thought I had made it all up.

Dear Suzanne,
I am glad to tell you what I know.

Your grandfather, my uncle, was an insurance salesman. He was a big man with a gentle disposition and a
smile for everyone.

It is impossible to explain to people who did not live
through the Depression what it was for a proud, independent man to find himself unable to provide for a
wife and four little children. Apparently he looked to
his life insurance as his only answer.

Sincerely,
Cousin M_____

A letter came from yet another cousin, the third who
had written to me from my mother's generation.

Dear Suzanne,

Our cousin, M_____ , asked me to tell you all I
knew about your family, happy, sad, gossipy. I could
never bring myself to tell you the tragedies of your family. I will now, though. I can only tell you what I remember. But what I tell you I know to be true. So here goes!

There were six children in the B_____ family who
were named after their grandmother, Goldie L_____ ,
your great-grandmother. [Good God! there was a
Goldie in my second novel!] I know nothing about this
grandmother except that she died young and had some
children who did not survive. My mother would never
talk about her life in Europe. They came from a farm in
Lithuania and the owner was supposedly kind to them.
But there were pogroms and my daughter, a psy-
chotherapist, feels that some of the sisters were raped.

Five of the children came with their father, Juda
B_____ , a very orthodox Jew, by boat in steerage to
Ellis Island around 1902. They traveled to Elmira, New
York, where another daughter lived, already married,
and set up house.

Your grandmother married your grandfather in
Elmira [Elmira!] in 1910. I don't remember too much
about your grandfather except that he must have been a
very fine man. I remember my father liked him very
much. He was in the life insurance business.

In 1930, a deep depression existed in the U.S. I believe his business had dwindled; he had a wife and four
children to support. To protect them so they could have
insurance to live on, he took his life by inhaling carbon
monoxide in the car in their garage. I just learned that
Elynore, your mother, discovered the body. I can't elaborate on this because I know little. I do know my uncle
was a gentleman, a kind and gentle man. He was very
tall and that's why his children were all so tall. I wish I
had known him more.

Your grandmother, my aunt, had a hard life. I liked
her more as the years went by. She was very modern
and a marvelous cook. I can't say she was sweet-tem-
pered but many things must have happened to her. To
live to see three wonderful children gone is more than a
human being should have to bear. She could sew and
she must have been very adept with her hands.

Your Aunt Goldyne was the loveliest of women. She
was almost as tall as Sylvia [the aunt who cared for me],

but built differently and beautiful. She had a cheerful disposition and was bright and gifted artistically. She could make wonderful gadgets, dressed with chic, and was an elegant woman. I was close to her. She married and taught school—grammar school—and she and her husband got some money together and bought a drug store. Her husband was not a pharmacist, so their overhead must have been very high. In those days schoolteachers were not allowed to have children. If they did, they were let go. One day Gold became very ill and died in the next two. I heard she had some kind of staphylococcus. They didn't have sulfa or penicillin then, which might have saved her life. However, just a few years ago some of Gold's former friends told me there was a mystery about her death. We will never know. She was thirty-one years old.

Sylvia you knew. She was a very sensitive person, extremely bright, very gifted. She sewed beautifully and was very original in cooking. She was different and everyone loved her.

Elynore, your mother. What a splendid woman. She was down to earth. She was very close to her brother. She and her mother seemed to have the same philosophy. I really didn't know your father. Your mother died at childbirth from what I understand was uremic poisoning [according to what I'd been able to wrench from my father, it was actually eclampsia, a sudden surge of blood pressure in labor]. I do remember hearing your father say when the cousins were gathered around the kitchen table that Elynore was having a hard pregnancy and she wondered if she was going to make it.

The boy, Paul, went into dentistry and then into the army. I've heard two versions of his death. One was told to me by his close friend who said Paul was in love with a native girl and the girl's boyfriend stabbed him to death. But when M——— asked me to write to you he said he had it on good authority that Paul had hung himself. Which is true?

Indeed, I asked myself, which is true, fiction or fact? And does it matter at all?

Tom had a phone message for me one evening when I came home late. "A woman called. She said she was your cousin Lonny. Someone you knew when you were a child."

It rang a bell. "You mean she's in town from the East Coast?"

"No, she lives in San Francisco."

I called the number and spoke with a smart, funny woman my age who had lived in the City for years. She was the education director at our planetarium. I'd probably seen her there when I'd taken the kids. Coincidentally—or maybe not; perhaps we will find someday that the developmental work of the late forties is to clear up the family mysteries—she had been searching for information about our family, as I had, and beating (in letters) on the same gray heads.

She and her husband came over for breakfast, and yes indeed, the minute I saw the cloud of red hair and the lively brown eyes I remembered! The tilt of the head, the sound of the voice, the long, long bones and white skin. I must have been five when I'd known her.

She was newly married at forty-eight, to a gentle physicist. She took my books home and read all night. Next day she called to tell me of things embedded there that she had recognized as part of our shared past.

"Using Goldie's name I understand. You know, all of our great-grandfather's children named their daughters some form of that name, so there are six that I know of in our mother's generation of cousins. And Elly, the mother of the troubled girl in *Out of Danger*—your mother was Elynore, wasn't she? But you know the rabbi on page so-and-so of *Coming Back Up*?" I remembered, vaguely. He was a minor character who only appeared once. "Did you know he has our grandmother's maiden name?"

Once more, I was rendered speechless.

"Not to mention that you have Paul in *Out of Danger*. And not to mention me." I hadn't thought of it until that moment. The protagonist in my first novel was Lonnie Mathias. There was something about the ring of the name that had always pleased me, but never once had I consciously thought of this cousin.

With a spin that I recognized easily as family humor, she said coyly, "That's Lonny, with a *y*. Could you just make sure you get the spelling right next time?"

I feel the satisfaction of a lifelong hunger, a craving finally sated. Like water cycling through the natural environment—as ocean, as vapor, as clouds, as rain—memory nurtures life, life nurtures memory, and both feed the beauty of the whole. What luck to stumble almost offhandedly on the chance to see in all its complexity the interwoven plait of past, present, memory, intellect, knowledge, intuition, playfulness, deep feeling, and—like Sappho's ribbon braided in—the writer's mysterious craft.

TO MARKET, TO MARKET

SEVENTEEN

Sour Grapes

Still, a person has to earn a living.

And my career as a novelist was lodged firmly in the mid-list—a place where literary novels languish quietly, watching the publishing rockets of the season soar and waiting in vain to be shot from cannons. Frightening to be a mid-lister in a blockbuster age. Doom-filled talk of the death of the novel and the final victory of television and the computer abound on the literary fringe, and I would guess that most such writers grind their teeth at night—when they are not sitting straight up in the dark in a financial panic. How long can I do this? we ask ourselves. How long before discouragement and exhaustion extinguish this little light of mine?

Fortunately family life does not permit the artist to take to her bed and sink slowly into neurasthenia. The recession of the nineties was gestating under the surface of Reaganomics, the acid of censorship and scorn was threatening the very role of artists in the overground culture, and still the children had to be fed and clothed, the phone bills—looking like rent bills of yore—had to be paid on time. My solitary literary walks gave way to walks with Tom in which we brainstormed on how to keep things working while holding anxiety levels down.

Still editing, I was exhausting myself in the outer edges of the publishing world. I vowed to transform myself once and for all into a sensible businesswoman. The idea was to embrace my multiple personalities—let the artist evolve as she would, unencumbered by financial expectations or responsibility, while the businesswoman kept things going.

Alas, I found a way.

I became a ghost.

"Your editor said *what*?"

"She told me that you had completely lost my voice."

I love to talk on the telephone. Sometimes, with fingers pasted to my computer keyboard for hour upon hour, amber letters lining up across the screen, I *live* for the telephone to ring. Each time it does, a gust of the wide world blows into my little office space, and I can lean back, watch the cows graze, check out my garden in a casual way, and "talk to New York."

But *this*. My author's words had given my stomach a jolt and my heart a jab, and suddenly the immediate future rose up to block out the view. I had counted on this book for more than half the year's income, and had been running down to the mailbox every day looking for the long over-due first half of the advance.

"Uh—" I said, reluctant to accept what I'd heard. "Uh, did she give you—*you* know, concrete particulars?"

"Nope. She just told me she thought you were all wrong for the project. You know I always suspected you were too literary, remember how I told you that?"

I remembered no such thing. I only remembered how grateful this particular fellow had been when I finally agreed to give up my silly plea to be credited as coauthor on the cover of the book and assume the role of ghost-writer. That distinction, by the way—cover credit versus no credit—might seem like a small thing to a nonwriter, but to a professional writer it can mean the difference be-tween an honest collaboration and a year or two of slowly building, poisonous resentment.

The distinction between collaborator and ghost is not well-known, but the blurring of the terms has ominous consequences for readers as well as writers:

Collaborating or co-writing is a legitimate joint pursuit by a person with something to say and a writer with the tools required to say it well. Both people are credited on the cover of the book for what they do. Sometimes a "with" links their names on the cover; sometimes their names ap-pear in different type sizes. Often the expert is referred to as the "author," or senior author, whereas the writer is called "the writer." Depending on the specifics of the deal, for a writer it can be nice work if you can get it. And unexpect-edly, once in a lifetime or so, a collaborative project can come along that is so *right,* with all the groundwork already laid and with intuition flowing effortlessly both ways, that it shows up the writer's trade for what it normally is: long, long silent stretches of solitary life so lonesome that, especially when it's working, even you, the writer, are barely there.

Ghostwriting, though, is an *il*legitimate, *in*authentic joint pursuit by a person with something to say (sometimes) and a writer with the tools required to say it (and sometimes to invent it). Only the former is credited on the cover of the book, and the latter is thanked in the acknowledgments for her support and editorial suggestions. And depending on the state of your finances at the time the chance arises, for a writer it may not be very nice work but, let's face it—aren't there times in every writer's financial life when it's necessary to turn a trick?

The answer must be *yes,* because judging from the anecdotal evidence that comes through my phone wire into my little farm porch, more and more books of every stripe are ghosted outright—or ghosted *de facto* by a freelance editor earning $15 an hour "just to tighten up the prose." This trend comes as a surprise to most book buyers, though I don't know why. We all know that many politicians and public figures hire others to write their speeches. We know, through the Milli Vanilli scandal (delightful to me), that singers might be ghosted on their records. We know that someone writes the news that our anchorpeople deliver. So why should it come as a surprise that our "authors"— many, many, many of our authors—fail to write their own books?

But it was the psychological, not the sociological, aspect of ghostwriting that had me in its grip at the moment. This fellow—who lived in an East Coast town I had never heard of and whom I had never met—held my financial security in the palm of his hand and had just made a fist. "She has another writer she thinks will take a more authoritative tone. I know you did your best, but it's, you know—a guy."

Oy, ghostwriting.

It can be a great way for writers to practice their craft while learning their way through the publishing industry.

Managed properly, it can be an adequate livelihood, with the potential—sporadically—for spectacular windfalls.

And above all it's a particularly great way to cut out your own liver, cook it with onions, and have it for breakfast every single working day for about two years per project.

Furthermore, you really can't complain, except to others who have given in to the same temptation to make a dishonest buck. If you complain, say, at a dinner party, that you just spent eight hours doing some of the hardest, most detailed, and maybe even the best work of your life under somebody else's name, the words hover over the dinner table like a heavy bunch of overripe globules orbited by fruit flies. Somebody's even liable to voice the question hanging there: "So if you hate it so much, why do you do it?"

Ghosting has consequences for readers as well as writers. By way of example: in a medical crisis some years ago, I found a book that gave me comfort. Because one of the worst things about disease for me was a strange inability to read, I was particularly grateful for the tone of this work—

it conveyed with directness, elegance, and above all a marked sensitivity to the dangers of generalization, things I needed to know and think about. I sank into the book and even began to make preliminary efforts to get in touch with the author.

And then, with a pang, it struck me. Who wrote this book, who *really* wrote it? Was it the woman on the cover, or was it someone like me, working uncredited in the background—interviewing the author, laboriously transcribing, digging through the concepts for a shape to the whole, and then drafting and redrafting the book? Quickly I turned to the acknowledgments page: "And to Chris Brown, for his wonderful suggestions, his unflagging editorial support, and his genius for organization."

Shit. A ghostwriter.

I laid the book aside.

You might argue that I was too hasty. Perhaps I should have taken that acknowledgment at face value—for a good editor can and often does make an immense contribution to a book without actually writing it. But having ghostwritten many, many nonfiction books, a seed of distrust was planted for me. And as everybody knows, there's nothing like distrust to poison a love affair, whether with a lover or the author of a book.

More than once I have told a client, in that brittle voice that to me expressed an imperfectly disguised cynicism, "It's my job to make you wake up in the morning, look into your mirror, and say, '*Damn*, I'm good.'"

Sound familiar?

You bet it does.

I've often drawn a parallel between ghosting for a living, especially for good money, and being a high-priced call girl. And I've told myself you can do it for money and still make love in your time off.

In the end, however, the parallel doesn't work, because the stereotype of an expensive prostitute has a superficial (though bogus) glamour to it, whereas ghosting is aptly named. Gradually, as the manuscript becomes a book, the ghost fades and disappears. By the time the author has been sent out on tour to the talk shows, the intense working relationship has dissolved, the money's been spent, and the ghost, if lucky, is exercising her way with words and her genius for organization on somebody else's raw material.

In short, the ghostwriter isn't a prostitute.

She—or he—is a wife.

My actual marriage is strictly egalitarian. Each of us does our fair share, each of us acknowledges or credits the other for every contribution to the family or draws attention to something about to slip by. But as a literary ghostwife, I was meek as a mouse.

Which, in that line of work, meant success. I ghostwrote many nonfiction books and found, to my building frustration, that they sold to publishers for sometimes quite dazzling sums. True, it is the *concept,* the big idea, that draws money in publishing, not the execution. Still, I was pouring time and energy into other people's bank accounts, while my own proposed efforts, like little matchgirls, went begging.

So, like the protagonist of my unborn novel still languishing on the shelf, I abandoned ghosting and became a runaway wife. Perhaps writing about it now so openly is analogous to Thelma and Louise speeding into the Grand Canyon, but as every ex-mouse will agree, equal credit— *cover credit*—and equal pay for equal work is worth the price.

And if that means sour grapes for dinner—well, honey, instead of turning up your nose, feel free to step out into the kitchen and fix yourself something enticing, delicious, nutritious, and beautiful on your own. Because there's more to making a meal than shopping and planning the menu.

And the only words worth eating are the truth.

EIGHTEEN

Reviewer-in-Recovery

I blush to admit: I'm a book reviewer-in-recovery. Don't get me wrong. I believe in book reviewing. Like most of my book friends, I love reading reviews and would miss them if they disappeared.

But reviewing books while you're writing ones of your own?

Very difficult.

You'd think I would have come to that conclusion gradually and naturally, but it hit me right in the face in a room full of people.

Two weeks before my first novel was to come out, I went alone to a local writer's book party. As I made my way through the throng to congratulate my friend, a woman shouted above the din, "So *you're* Suzanne Lipsett. You gave my book the worst review I received in the whole country. And in my hometown paper yet. Thanks a *lot.*"

The roar of the party diminished and I felt fifty pairs of eyes turn my way.

Luckily I remembered exactly what I'd written about this woman's book, and privately I uttered a prayer of thanks that I hadn't wrapped up with a zinger, a one-liner that had been just too good to pass up.

"Gee, you know," I said, "if that was the worst you got, your book must have done very well. I wouldn't call that a bad review by any stretch. I really liked your book—a lot."

"So why did I go to bed for two weeks?"

"Really? You did?"

"Yes, really."

"I don't see why. I thought I made it clear you did a great job—"

"Well, maybe I overreacted—" she said, and looked off across the room, just a hint of defensiveness surfacing.

"No, no, that's not what I meant. I just thought—" So *I* got defensive, but in fact we both knew my review had been tepid, enthusiasm for the book conspicuous in its absence, and just for the merest instant I thought if we continued to flummox around about this, one of us could wind up severely wounded. But she managed to pull herself together and smile, graciously attempting to bring the exchange of poison darts to an end. Just then, however, someone called to her across the crowd, "Hey, L_____ , are *you* going to review Suzanne's novel when it comes out?"

An expressionless man—I remember him as bearlike and formidable—with his arms crossed on his chest, stepped forward. "No, *I'm* going to do it," he growled—or at least he growled it in my recollection of the event. The husband. Eeek. I made a hasty retreat and drove the forty miles home from the City, my mind whirring with the terror of rejection.

When I finally wrote my first novel, at age forty, my life came together and made sense. Everything that had seemed pointlessly difficult, or pointlessly intense, or directionless and arbitrary fed the effort and became, or tried to become, art.

I had had two children by then, and for me the joy of producing a book was analogous to pregnancy in almost every way—except I didn't need a man to do it.

In this context I understand that rejection hurts so deeply because authentic art is conceived in love.

And that, of course, is its power.

I don't mean to say that all loved work will be openly received.

But I do know that the love of the work—loving thinking it, writing it, rewriting it, polishing it—is what keeps it alive in the face of rejection, casual criticism, or indifference. If the work stays alive—and some doesn't; some dies—it stays alive because its creator loves it, *not* because its receivers do.

Indeed rejection has much to teach writers—and a good thing too, since it's always present or potentially present in a creative artist's life.

It is the stone against which we sharpen our pens.

It can take off our skin, but it gives us a chance to measure the strength of our commitment.

But even deeper than that, the rough stone of rejection can scrape through the surface of our work and reveal the depth of our truth.

Truth might hide out, but it doesn't go away. And the love of bringing it to light via art may lie dormant, but I don't think it can die.

Now, instead of writing reviews, I write letters of condolence to writers I see trashed in the press. I don't have to have read their books to feel a clang in my chest at the sight of a one-liner aimed at their work. I've never subscribed to any religious beliefs, but I find that, yes, I do believe in an exclusive little literary hell. There, but for learning to let dogs lie and die a natural death, burn I.

NINETEEN

Shoot Me Again

I dial the number of my publisher in New York. I'm delighted to start the week with a question or two regarding my own book project, rather than having to untangle somebody else's editorial troubles. This is my first novel. It's been a long time coming, the publisher is really very prestigious—frankly I'm flattered. And fantastically excited. Even proud.

"So-and-So's office." The editor's assistant sounds young enough to be the boss's child, in for the day and playing receptionist.

"Is So-and-So available?" I ask.

"Who can I say is calling?"

"Suzanne Lipsett."

"Susan, ah—could you spell it?"

Just a slight pause, only the wee-est constriction of the throat.

"Yes, it's Suzanne, with a z, L-I-P-S-E-T-T."

"L-I-P—?"

As in anaphylactic shock, my throat grows tighter. My book has been through editorial and is scheduled for publication in the upcoming season. Granted, it's a "small" novel, but an invisible one? I struggle to swallow and spell my name again.

"And you're calling about—?"

Oh, shit. I'm defeated. I wonder how long I can sleep and still work on the chapter I'd planned to finish today if I crawl away from my desk and back into bed for a nap.

"About my book," I whisper.

"Your book?"

"My novel." I clear my throat, begin to speak, clear my throat and find an assertive tone. "Which you are publishing in the spring." I'm horrified: it came out like a whine.

"Oh. Oh, really? Title?"

Dead.

Of disappointment and embarrassment.

It will take me three weeks to shake loose of the questions that are slowly filling my mind, like mud oozing out of the ground. Whatever had given me the idea I could be a novelist? Why am I stealing time from my children if my publisher doesn't even know my name? What on earth am I getting out of the struggle, in a time when six- and seven-figure advances are the standard of success, to forge a writer's identity and stay in print?

One more question forms in direct response to the assistant's smart-mouth tone: Who do I think I am?

The writer's path winds upward, toward a mountain range lost in clouds. Just when you think you've achieved the peak you've been struggling toward, another mountain—just one more mountain!—is revealed to be looming on the other side. When you're writing your first stories, it's getting one published. When you've gotten one published, it's perfecting your form. For me the next step was daring a novel. And the peak after that was publication. Still more rugged mountaintops loom in the distance (the Anapurna of all published writers has the ominous name of "Staying in Print"). I suppose the reason I never learned the lay of the land beforehand was that it was all I could do to keep to the upward path.

So I worked and worked my throat until I could swallow what I had to, and then continued doggedly up the path. And since my early climbs, I've taken pleasure in finding ways to alert aspiring writers a step or two behind me to the dangers and shocks up ahead for most. (Not everyone sustains them, as everybody knows. There *are* those daredevils who, when it comes time to jump off a cliff, hurl themselves, glide, catch a current, and soar—and it's thrilling to see, even if for a second you're chilled by their shadows.) Perhaps it's the same for any pursuit, but the way is strewn with those who have fallen off the path—not for want of writing talent, not for lack of stories to tell (though in both cases there are those, of course), but out of sheer discouragement at the steepness of the climb.

It was October 1991, nearly a decade since I jumped off my first cliff. Worse luck for me, my career as a fiction writer corresponded with the ascendancy of the block-buster mentality. I counted myself lucky that I was still on the path.

In the mail I received an announcement from the Author's Guild, a professional organization for writers. The guild was sponsoring a day-long conference in Los Angeles to launch a West Coast branch. According to the flyer, the objective was quite consciously to begin to break the stranglehold of New York publishing on the aesthetic and economic lives of writers in other parts of the country. Yes, yes, yes, I intoned, and scrawled off a check.

Los Angeles was blindingly hot. The conference was at a country club on Sunset Boulevard. The setting couldn't have been more beautiful or, in the understated way of wealth that takes itself for granted, more intimidating. You could slip outside behind one of the twenty-foot panels of gauzy drapes to a wide, tiled balcony overlooking a downy golf course. Wet mown grass obliterated the smell of traffic beyond the long curving driveway on Sunset, acre upon acre of city shone white and toylike in the morning sun, and beyond it the Pacific Ocean was a wide band of silver curving away. Not every morning, but today for sure, the powerful fantasy of Los Angeles had come together like a celluloid dream.

I signed in, stuck my name tag on, and looked around at the other registrants.

Eyes darted at my tag, then away, then chest-high on someone else. Paper coffee cups were lifted to hide others' tags, then tentatively dropped to reveal them, then lifted again. Here and there clumps of writers stood talking. For something to do, since I didn't know anyone, I sat on the couch and ate a Danish while I watched—and felt something in the air I couldn't put my finger on. The hall quickly crowded up—there were several hundred participants—but not with friendliness and good cheer. I sensed a nervous quality, a shyness, I hadn't expected.

A few minutes remained before the opening panels, so I attempted a little light banter. "What brings you here?" I asked the woman of about forty who was sharing my couch sipping coffee from a gold-ringed china cup. She looked extremely professional—she wore a suit and hose and heels. I let my eyes flick over her name tag and alarm broke through her reserve. "Oh," she said, "you'll never have heard of *me*. I've been out of print for twelve years."

I smiled and withdrew to my Danish, but on my right, balanced a little tipsily on a very elegant brocaded chair, was a rumpled man in a tweed jacket, grumbling in my direction. He seemed to take my glance his way as an invitation to complain. "I don't recognize a single name here. I mean, you know, the *names*—where are they? I guess the last thing they need is another conference, right? I mean, if you were making a million bucks a book, would *you* be paying sixty-five dollars to listen to a bunch of literary types whine about their bank accounts?"

"What if I told you I *am* making a million dollars a book?" I joked.

"I'd ask you what the hell you were doing here on a day like this. On a day like this you ought to be in Majorca.

And besides, I wouldn't believe you because I don't recognize your name. And I read *all* the trash writers—*all*. Stuff's so bad but I have to. That's what I want to be—a trash writer. I just can't get *bad* enough, that's the trouble with me."

He was a professional kvetch with a Brooklyn whine himself, but he ended with a lift to his chin and a hint of a smile, and I saw that he was enjoying himself immensely. We were a crowd of writers, after all. You could say *all* the unsayables—"mid-listed," "orphaned," "rejected," "between agents," *any*thing.

The first session, on agents, was standing room only out by the tennis courts, and we could watch the early morning players volleying as the four agents at the front gave their breathless spiels. If there had been a mood of reticence in the lobby around the registration table, there was a kind of communal glower in the overflow audience. Maybe not everyone had their arms crossed and their eyes slitted, but the sense of "Oh, yeah?" was overpowering. The reason wasn't hard to spot—the agents were the only ones who looked like they belonged in the swank tennis club setting. I wouldn't say the rest of us looked dowdy, but recycling consciousness seemed to have governed our choices in clothes.

Here was a room full of people who had spent their days layered in their children's sweats and old flannel shirts from the sixties staring into their computer screens and forgetting, every day, to plan for dinner. Here was a group that lived for the phone to ring and went through crisis therapy in the effort not to call their agents too soon, not to gain the reputation of "difficult author" or—death!—outright pain in the ass. Here was a roomful of independent minds whose individualism in outlook and voice was their stock in trade, a great number of whom had remained in non-productive, if not completely defunct, relationships with their agents for years and years and years. I venture to guess that a large proportion of the group in that room was hoping to find new agents on the panel. And of course the four women dressed to the teeth and smiling excitedly at us from the table up front were there to pick the flowers, such as we were.

Each gave her talk, marched out her successes, rationalized her disappointments, and begged us to understand the agents' plight in the publishing process—they had the indescribable excitement of discovering new talent, presenting it in exactly the right way to exactly the right editor, and making the publishing deal. By and large, they missed out on the extended fulfillment of creation that was the writer's lot. The agent's fun ended with the money.

If I were choreographing this scene for a musical comedy set in the publishing world, at this sentiment I would have had all two hundred and fifty assembled writers recross their arms, recross their legs, and hunker down lower in their chairs. Agents and writers are destined to stare at each other in distrust down the ages. Only the fact that a literary agent is one of my closest friends saves me, I think, from the utter and mutual incomprehension that seems to characterize many agent-writer relationships (and my pal and I, though tempted now and then, do not dare to risk our friendship by signing each other up).

With an anecdote within an anecdote, I threaten to turn this account into a shaggy dog story, but this particular story captures the difficulties perfectly in a quick and dirty way. After a long, difficult, stormy, but highly productive relationship with an agent, we parted ways and I had a short-lived relationship with another. Briefly this second agent courted me: he petted, he licked, he smoothed my fur like an expert handler and, yes, I rolled over on my back and waved my paws.

We dined, we each liked what we saw and heard, we agreed to team up—and from that point on, it was a quick slide down into the same old confusion of crashing realities. To make a short story shorter, one nasty phone call made it clear that we would no longer be working together, and the honeymoon was terminated there and then. Some weeks later a writer on my gossip tree said to me, "So-and-So told me he fired you."

"He *what?*" I could feel my eyes popping. "He *fired* me?"

"That's what he said."

"Well, I'd say it was a question of who got there first. But how does an agent fire a writer? Didn't he work for me?"

"I think he probably meant that he was building a stable and he didn't want you in it, so he asked you to leave."

So I wasn't an adored kitten but a used-up old mare. "To keep the metaphor pure," I mused into the phone, "why didn't he just take me out back and shoot me?"

So the agents pitched themselves to the writers and the writers crossed their legs. At the end of the session, most of the writers in the room probably felt even more alienated from the business half of the writing game than before the session began.

If they, like I, entertained the suspicion that wheeling and dealing in the literary marketplace often came to nothing, they were in for confirmation at the second morning panel: "On Being a Writer in Los Angeles." On this panel were two writers who had impressed and moved me deeply in the seventies—Clancy Sigal, author of *Weekend in Dinlock,* and Hubert Selby, author of *Last Exit to Brooklyn.* Said Sigal about the course of his long literary career, "In a way I'm like a whore, but I go where the money isn't. I wouldn't have been a rich call girl. I would have been like all the Molly O's I grew up with on the West Side of Chicago, who ended up sticking their heads in the ovens. They couldn't make a dime. And I don't go where the money is, I go where the energy is."[1]

In London, he went on, writers are respected. "Writing is not a respectable occupation here in Southern California, unless you're connected to the film business, which essentially, I'm not . . . essentially, I'm like a woman here. I'm invisible and transparent, and my work doesn't matter to the basic community. . . . I find that I am treated as a woman by my men friends simply because I'm a novelist."

I had to ponder the layers of those remarks. If a writer of Sigal's stature thought of himself at best as a woman doing woman's work and at his lowest moments as a suicidal hooker, what on earth did that make me, who didn't have to *fail* to be a woman and who hoped somehow to make a living at what I did? I felt the writers around me shift uncomfortably in their chairs.

But if Sigal's remarks set us all to pondering, Selby's could have been a call to slit our throats. "Eight years ago," said this longstanding literary hero of mine who had had the inner fortitude to describe a world that the mainstream culture dismissed with contempt and disgust, "I was on welfare. A couple of years ago, I was cleaning toilet bowls to make a living. And I write because I have no choice. If I had a choice, I certainly would not do what I do. But I have no choice. And that's the way it is. So, maybe my attitude is all right. It helps me stay alive."

Oh. He had an endearing way of speaking and a heart-wrenching story to tell, but as he spoke so diffidently I began to wonder whether it might not have been a better choice to trot out to the back of that agent's barn to be shot. Although the ensuing panel discussion was riveting and lively, when it was over the audience remained planted, arising moments later only slowly, as if during the panel discussion their pants had slowly filled with wet sand.

In fact, though the setting was meant to be uplifting and the intentions of the organizers high, it was hard to imagine a more depressed and dispirited bunch than the attendees at that conference. Judging from the exchanges in the panels, the murmuring gossip in the women's room, and the lunch-table conversation, these were well-published writers who had expected that, once established with one or two books, they would be able to stay in print, if not make their livings with their pens. But for most the gaps between books were intolerably long, and for many the prospects for publishing again seemed to be fading. To me, the horrible thing was that they—we— seemed to take the full blame. The cliché has it that depression is anger turned inward, and in volleys of self-parody and wry self-deprecation, the writers at my lunch table seemed ready to beat themselves up verbally for not being good enough.

True to her history, Erica Jong took to the podium and challenged all that. If her classic *Fear of Flying* had rattled the culture by giving voice to her female protagonist's sexual fantasies, her keynote address at the Author's Guild conference was designed to break our concentration on our navels and make us take a cool look at the outside world.

"You probably know Voltaire's remark," she began. "'Nothing is to be expected from the practice of literature but contempt if one fails and sheer hatred if one succeeds.' If our books hit the bestseller list, our fellow authors *loathe* us. If our books don't hit the bestseller list, our publishers ignore us. . . . Here we are in a profession where we can never do *anything* right."

I could feel myself sigh, and feel my table partners relax, as truth blew into the room like a breeze off the ocean.

Then she called us "software," the software of the giant corporate conglomerates that have been buying up the publishing industry over the last decade, altering it radically by pulling up the old rules and laying down their own. But unlike the software that run our computers, she said, writers are software with brains. Though, despite her bad-girl rep, Erica Jong was far too polite to point it out, the implication was that, regarding the *business* of writing, those brains were not yet in gear. "We never think of the *economics*. . . . We just go into a depression, or drink too much, or visit our shrinks—"

Tepid laughter.

But then she began to rouse the crowd.

"We want the rights of individual creators to prevail, partly because we have to make a living, partly because we understand how hard it is to be an individual creator, but also because we understand that the written word is the beginning of all culture.

"We also have a basic sense of fairness. Why shouldn't we be paid for our work if the paper manufacturers are paid for their work? Why should we always work for love *alone?* Our work is intangible, but our bills are not. I want the needs of writers to be recognized. . . . Have I talked a lot about power issues and bread and butter issues? Well— that's not because intellectual issues don't matter, but because we must have bread on the table *as well as* ideas. I think we have waited too long to get to this point. There are many other worthy organizations that deal with intellectual issues. And other groups deal with free expression and writers in prison in distant lands. But economic censorship here in the U.S. is also a powerful form of oppression. If we cannot live by our work, we cannot continue creating it.

"I am also concerned with fair public relations for authors. I want to show the world that most authors have to take a day job to survive. Naturally they are not the ones who get most of the publicity. The average writer makes less than $10,000 a year. The average writer does not have an agent to X out all those obnoxious clauses in the boilerplate. The average writer works as a university professor, a therapist, a reporter, a screenwriter, or a technical writer in order to create a novel."

A collective rustle seemed to indicate mass agitation, perhaps suppressed excitement. The "average writer" *does?* seemed to pose itself in eyes around the room. You mean, I'm not the only one at this table

- whose beloved offering never went into paperback?

- whose last book sank like a stone?

- whose original editor is long gone and whose current editor treats her like Cinderella?

- whose editorial assistant never, *never!* remembers her name?

"Writers write the books that eventually change the world. Writers are the people on whom the next revolution in consciousness depends. Change starts with books and then filters down to other forms of media. . . .

"A culture that destroys its writers, that impoverishes its writers, that makes its writers feel defeated is a culture that cannot survive" [my italics].

The rabble was roused, the audience was on its feet. I suppose nobody heard me, but it was two months away from an election year and I meant it when I chanted, "Erica for President"!

Now, I ask you, demands that audacious inner voice. Why go through it all? Why work so hard? Why *write*?

Somehow the time is right, and answers boil up easily from all that's gone before:

Because life can hurt and, properly practiced, writing doesn't.

Because ideas are as nothing—mere vapors on the wind—without form.

Because the present can so completely obliterate the past, causing those who are buried there to disappear forever.

Because writing heals and then goes beyond, to make something new from the old.

And because, darling, honestly: it is the one thing I can do.

---

1. All comments from the conference speakers are quoted from an account in the Author's Guild *Bulletin* (Summer 1992).

TWENTY

Full Circle

One of my few truly prized possessions is a hardback copy of *The Golden Apples,* by Eudora Welty, inscribed to me by the author. It reads, in part, "in memory of the Jackson visitation," and she wrote it to me in her living room after admitting how guilty she felt at letting the splendor of her mother's garden fade.

"She grew flowers for cutting and filled this house," said Eudora. "Oh, it was *glorious.*"

It was my one foray out of the publishing world. I was the production assistant—"the girl"—on a documentary film crew making a series of half-hour films for the Public Broadcasting System called *The Writer in America.* I was hopeless at the collaborative art of filmmaking and nearly expired on location five or six times a day, fatally bored and glazed over waiting through the interminable set-up of shots for something, *any*thing, to happen. Plugs, cords, surge protectors, changing bags, cartridges, lenses, viewing gizmos, batteries, duct tape, and those dozens of formidable metal suitcases—all these were pure sex objects to the film-struck, but the mere sight of the mountainous piles of things we had to move from airport to motel, motel to location, and back again triggered narcolepsy in me.

Still, I was good at the preparation. For this film portrait, I had read several collections of Ms. Welty's stories and several novels—the whole film crew had. And I was a good listener. I hoped I was a reassuring female presence for Ms. Welty when the three-man crew and I invaded her wonderful old family house in Jackson. In the long correspondence that had preceded our visit, she had been terribly modest and was reticent to agree to be filmed. And in the sleepy towns we visited along the Mississippi River, filming "atmosphere," one living Welty character after another echoed her misgivings, but with a sharper spin. "Oh, Eudora Welty," a wattle-necked, hairsprayed old lady would snap at us across the counter in a diner or a hardware store. "Now why would anybody want to make a movie about *her?*"

The reason became clear on our first day of filming—so clear, in fact, that simply being present, remaining as still as I could, changed and enriched my life.

We were all nervous, because she was. She was nearly seventy then, though a hearty seventy. After finally agreeing to participate, she had invited us in to film her in her own home, where she had grown up the well-loved child of her parents, as she would later describe so gracefully in *One Writer's Beginnings.* She was not in the least shy and certainly had not the slightest resemblance to a Southern belle or a crabby eccentric, though both stereotypes had been invoked in our side trips out into the countryside to film Spanish moss and porch-sitters along the Delta. She laughed as easily as you'd imagine the writer of "Why I Live at the P.O." to laugh. And her passion was high—the evening before that first filming she recollected for us the night that black civil rights activist Medgar Evers was killed. "I stayed up all night, thinking," she told us. "And though I never met him, I *knew* Medgar Evers that night. And I knew his mother too."

We fussed in the living room while she went upstairs to get ready—fussed and fanned. In this room, she had told us, she laid out the pages of her stories and novels on the floor. She would try out first one order, then another, and then use straight pins to connect them up.

I was in terror of dropping something as I moved things here and there under the director's guidance. The cine-matographer squinted and grumbled into the camera, peri-odically emerging to peer at the room before hunching back over the eyepiece again. The sound man taped and retaped wires to the floor. When Eudora finally came down, she was wearing a beautiful, bright yellow dress. As the cinematog-rapher later remarked, all four of us had underestimated her tremendously, because she had the presence and composure of a great woman who knows the value of her work.

And the voice of a born storyteller, compelling, dra-matic, and soft.

She sat in a chair and read "A Worn Path," about an old, old raisin of a back-country granny walking to the city to fetch medicine for her little grandson, whose throat was closing up. He had drunk lye.

The camera hummed quietly; we were motionless. Miraculously, the story ran comfortably within the seventeen-minute reel length. And her very first words had changed the room. What had begun as a work crew became a circle of listeners connected by that rhythmic Southern voice.

She finished, raised her face, and her eyes filled up. "Oh, isn't that just beautiful?" she asked us, tears sliding down her cheeks.

So many threads of meaning in such a tight little knot of experience. It took me years to tease them all out. The truths conveyed in those seventeen minutes and the small drama of their conclusion, as far as I succeeded in separating them, were these:

- that once you make a thing it can detach from you and enter the world on its own terms, separate from you forever;

- that such detachment can allow you to love and appreciate it for itself, not simply because you made it;

- that, with regard to the truth, the distinction between the reality of fiction and the reality of "fact" is of little consequence;

- and that if they have found a vein to the truth, writers can only grow deeper and better with age.

Many years later, and about a month ago, two dear book friends and I decided to defy American custom and draw attention to the fact that we had decidedly entered that zone of invisibility called middle age. We threw a Late Bloomers party and invited the women friends in their forties and fifties we wanted to introduce to one another. Many of these women, we sensed, had begun new ventures or intensified old efforts in their late forties. We wanted to celebrate those efforts and, in the spirit of the time, do some gossiping.

Being far from sorry to be forty-eight, after riding the whitewater of cancer, I didn't think much of our concept except to look forward to a party at the beach. But I called up a lovely young Frenchwoman I knew and told her I'd like to make her an exception to our late-forties criterion. She was a very smart, stylish anthropologist who had been educated in Europe and had become an ardent feminist. I thought she'd be particularly interested in what was happening with the first rank of feminism's second wave twenty-five years after we had begun to smash old definitions of "women's work."

"Oh, no!" she answered when I told her what was up. "All those ladies will just *hate* me."

"*Hate* you?"

"But of course. Because I am young. They will be too jealous."

It was an unfortunate response, and an impulsive one, I could tell. I don't doubt that my friend regretted it as soon as it was out of her mouth. I decided to forgive it but I could not forget it.

A month went by and I called her again.

"You know, we have to talk."

"About—?"

"About myself and my friends. About becoming fifty. About refusing to disappear. About insight gained through experience. About the value of doing something for so many years that you are really good at it, and owe it its proper due." I was in danger of haranguing, but I couldn't quite stop. "About respect—"

"You mean because I said—?"

"I don't think it's your fault. I think you just don't know. I think we haven't really made ourselves plain. You know a lot about the challenge to the old models, but I don't really think you *know*—"

She felt horrible, of course, and offered to bring a French apple pie.

The weather at the beach was glorious, and judging from the food our guests had deposited on the table and the laughter and lively conversation all around, the party was a wild success. But Cecile, a fiery novelist with little patience for small talk, suddenly took it upon herself to break up the small groups of women scattered about the wide-open beach house and herd us all out into the patio, a square at the center of the house surrounded by four walls but open to the sky. "There are far too many interesting people here," cried Cecile, "and I'll never be able to talk to them all. Come on, come on, outside where we can hear each other. Come out and tell us all about yourselves."

My heart sank. The idea was for Marie, Candice, and me to meet each other's friends, but we certainly didn't want to put anybody on the spot. Nevertheless, Cecile was a potent force, and we all filed out obediently to settle around the wooden walls of the little courtyard. There were about thirty-five of us, all of us in that group that used to be called—snidely, I thought—women of a certain age. A circle of women in a courtyard. With all the hats and summer clothes, it made a nice picture.

Cecile urged us on a little more, but not much, and one at a time we told our stories. Had husbands or lovers, sons or daughters been present, they might have been disappointed or even hurt to find they were not mentioned at all. One by one, by unspoken agreement, we told our stories of work. Writers, printers, businesswomen, professors, students, teachers, photographers, therapists, filmmakers, master gardeners, committed full-time householders—these were gifted women, and they clearly welcomed the opportunity to track their progress in identifying their true work and integrating it with the many other strands of their lives. Not one of these women reflected the conventional timetable. Far from slowing down and coasting as they approached or began their fifties, many, like me, were just starting to assess their potential and find their direction.

As one of the hosts, I spoke last. I recounted my story, but found it impossible to express a building emotion. I had bumbled and struggled and stayed my course to make myself into a writer, kicking and hollering with frustration at the endless obstacles. I had fought the common expectation that you blaze up early and start to die out about now, but I had harbored regret in my heart that I wasn't farther along the path.

Listening to these women, though—many of us gray-ing, all of us casting a wider shadow than we once did—I thought of Eudora Welty on her hands and knees on her living room floor, pinning together her stories and her life. The gifted women in this circle had lived a great deal and had, with intention, been forging a new way. Constantly, even compulsively, we had been studying the various pieces of our lives, turning them this way, turning them that way, then pinning together a version to try out.

Sitting in a circle telling each other our stories—it felt like the first step toward telling them to the world.

"Splendid!" cried Cecile. "Splendid! Now—" imperi-ously—"you may resume eating."

So, with most of us circling fifty, and with nothing to lose and everything to gain, we did.

End Note

Now all that's said—that's one version, at least—and tomorrow I will take up my novel.

This morning on my walk I stopped at the wall of blackberries to pick and eat.

I pulled long grass on my side of the fence for three horses and a mule.

I passed the spot where, unaccountably, a ground owl once built her nest on a curve in the road and fiercely defended it against oncoming cars all season; the spot where we saw a pair of foxes in the headlights; the spot where one night we nearly slammed into a black cow; the spot where a man crashed into a tree, leaving a scar, and died.

I avoided the spot where a dead possum moldered—and two places where Tom and I had argued bitterly and had had to walk home separately on the empty road.

I stood in the shadow of the eucalyptus trees, where one dusk five owls, all of different species, glided out to hunt.

Then I walked on, gazing out over the valley, and an old, old phrase dropped into my mind like an ember from a long-burning log. The quick flare of beauty—the glory of the language in the glory of the landscape—made me slow my step.

Listen to the words, I told myself. No, I mean really *listen* to the promise in those simple, timeless words:

"Once, my children. Once, upon a time . . . "